Character is Contagious

...and this is how you catch it!

Raymond C. Evans

DEDICATION

This book is dedicated to my mother and father, who gave me my first start, took care of me and sent me out into the "big wide world". My parents were the first to mold my personality and character into whatever I was to become.

ACKNOWLEDGMENTS

Thanks to all who helped me along life's exciting journey. Thanks to all who contributed help in writing this book, thanks especially to my wife Joy and my two daughters Kathy and Susie for all their help of expertise and encouragement.

My utmost appreciation and thanks I extend also to all those people who have taken part in the molding of any good qualities in my personality that I may possess. I wish to thank all my family and friends and all the characters I have known who are mentioned in this book.

FOREWORD

More than anything else in our lives that mold us are the personalities and characters of those with whom we associate. It starts with our fathers and our mothers, our sisters and our brothers when we are just tots still messing our diapers and no doubt, it will be our nurses in the end who will be molding us as we are once again messing our diapers. Everyone we meet is molded by their own tragedies, their own friends and associates, their drudgeries and their glories.

When we are young, our lives are akin to the writing of a book. We don't know for sure how the story is going to unfold at first and it's a real struggle to fill the pages. When we get older it is much easier to understand our lives because we become *"readers"* instead of *"writers"*. We have our memories to look back on and it's a lot easier to read the book about things known than to write about the unknown. When we are young, we have the worries of the future. When we are old, we relish in the glories of the past.

Yes, we are indeed a part of everything we have ever heard or seen, a part of every place we've ever been and a part of every person we've ever met. Of course, we also have had an impact on everyone with whom we have had contact. Our personalities, just like the measles and the plague, have been spread around to everyone we have ever met, and like the measles and the plague, our personalities are contagious.

Once, I too was young, like the writer full of wonder. Would I be rich? Would I be famous? Would I have children? Would I live to be old, as some youngsters think I am now, and perhaps write a book? Now, at the age of 69, I can look back and be a "*reader*" and "*write*" about my life, however mediocre, but, still full of rich memories. This is my moment. This is my chance to speak out. This is my chance to make a fool of myself once again to all who read these pages, my chance to remember and reminisce about all those characters and personalities who shaped my life into what it is today.

For most of us, our personality and character is shaped by our work. Ask any man his name and he's also apt to tell you what he does for a living. Ask a woman the same question and she's apt to tell you how many children she has.

It's not only the characters and personalities of others that shape our lives, but also I believe, our genetic makeup as well. If this is true, think of the ramifications. It would mean that our personalities would be shaped by our ancestors associations and relationships as well. Think of the magnitude of it all! It's just possible that our personalities, in part at least, could be shaped by someone who lived in other centuries, whose histories we have long forgotten. I've met a few people along the way who I thought may have resembled Atilla the Hun, perhaps genetic imprints were the reason for that after all. It has been my good fortune though, to have met and rubbed shoulders with many more people who were great to be associated with, good, kind and generous people. It is those good, kind and generous people who I hope have imprinted some of their character and personalities on me.

I will use some fictitious names throughout this story to protect the innocent (and the guilty). Many names will just be representative of the various nationalities and backgrounds. I have had the good fortune to have met a lot of interesting characters, it is my hope that at least some of their good traits may have rubbed off on me.

Chapter I

Family

The year 1932 was the year that I was born, but if you were to observe our family from the perspective of today, you would think that we were living in the time of the eighteen hundreds. Sure, there were a few things that were nineteen hundred era. We had a radio, for instance, and an old Nash car that my father could drive to town occasionally for groceries. The trips to town were mostly for staples such as flour, sugar etc. and perhaps some hardware that my father couldn't produce on his forge and anvil. Almost every-thing else needed was produced on the forty-acre stump ranch or ordered from the Sears & Roebuck or Montgomery Ward catalogs.

It was these catalogs that first introduced us to the idea of recy-cling as the old ones were used for toilet paper in the outhouse out back. They worked quite well actually, especially the index pages, which were the softest. The pretty glossy pages weren't as good but they were all used and all the old timers used to say that if the family was healthy, they would be in the pages of the *horse harnesses* by spring. They were always the last pages of the catalog.

Our family was soon to have electricity in its simplest forms. It was installed in 1935, I believe, and was simply one plug- in receptacle in the whole house and a wire hanging down from the ceiling in each room with a light bulb and plug receptacle both operated by a pull-chain. There was no refrigerator, range, water heater, clothes washer or dryer or any other device that used very much electrical current so it was really quite adequate for lighting. The clothes washer was a wringer type that was powered by a two cycle, "kick start" very smoky and noisy gasoline engine. The electrical installation was all quite primitive but still a large improvement over the gaslights and kerosene lamps that my mother struggled with every day.

The house was heated by the always hungry wood heater and the wood-burning cook stove, which also heated the water. A tank stood behind the cook stove, which provided the only hot water source. It worked pretty well actually, but only when there was a hot fire in the stove. In summer, if you wanted hot water, you also had to live in a very hot house.

The radio was a marvel to behold. It operated with a truck battery on the floor. It had a separate speaker about the size of a modern wastebasket and a console about 10 inches high and about three feet long. It had several dials and gauges on the front and the whole contraption must have weighed about 50 pounds. We could only receive one channel on it even with a very large antenna wire over the house. Even then, it was mostly static, but we thought it was a great invention anyway.

The main reason, I guess, that our living was so much like the 1800-era was that all the farming was done with horse teams. Horse team farming dictates that you are surrounded with old-fashioned implements and tools as well as old-fashioned methods. My dad was somewhat of a blacksmith also, so a lot of the tools were hand-made with a forge and anvil as well as almost all of the repairs.

9

The isolation of the area we lived in contributed also to our primitive way of living. We were isolated by the Eel river for one thing, the only road to town crossed over the river on a "summer bridge". This bridge was under water for much of the time during the winter and many times it would wash out in the first high water from the winter rains. When it washed away many times it would be getting along well into the summer before the bridge builders and their "pile drivers" could rebuild it. The long distance from any major town was also an isolating factor. It was at least thirty miles or more to any stores that would afford economical shopping. It wouldn't have made very much difference anyway as there certainly wouldn't have been very much money to spend. Our parents should be given great credit for how well they kept our large family of ten kids well fed and clothed.

You had to be self sufficient to survive. Fortunately for us the land was bountiful. The hills surrounding our little farm had deer, rabbits and quail. The river had fish. The open areas and fields that surrounded all the brush land had the most luscious, juicy blackberries that you could ever imagine. In the fall season, about late September, the smokehouse would be absolutely full of smoked salmon, which were pulled out of the river in that time of year. As soon as the salmon was cured really well, it was packed away in the pantry to make way for the one or two hogs that were butchered in late October. I can almost smell that smoked salmon hanging in the smokehouse as I think about it and those big slabs of bacon too. It makes my mouth water just to think about it.

We didn't have a refrigerator before 1941, or a freezer until about 1950, so prior to that time all the food for winter had to be canned and preserved in the summer. There was a whole storeroom full of canned goods from the garden, wild blackberries and applesauce, peaches, pears, cherries, prunes and plums from the trees. We had fall apples that would last all winter. Big, old, ugly-looking but delicious "*hubbard squash*", potatoes and onions were stored in bins in a cool place in the horse barn. Carrots and parsnips would last all winter left in the ground. I hated the parsnips, but loved the carrots and the rest of it.

There wasn't any pretty plastic packaging loaded with advertising on any of that food as there is today. Sometimes you might bite a worm in half if you weren't careful biting into one of those big, juicy apples.

We thought we were living high. The fact that you had to *shoot* it, *gut* it, *pick* it or *pluck* it made you appreciate it all the more. Some of that food was downright tasty. I can still, after all these years have passed, imagine the sight of those little fat quail coming out of the oven, their little drumsticks all lined up like a picket fence and just the right amount of gravy. *Ooh*, I can almost smell the aroma now and those biscuits my mother used to make; it just makes my mouth water. I haven't had anything like it since and to think that we assumed we were just poor folks.

Chapter 2

My Maternal Grandparents

My maternal grandparents were characters. Their lives were shaped by events that we would find to be almost unimaginable. If we could understand it at all, perhaps it would clarify their impact on my mother's character as described in the following chapter. They were getting quite elderly by the time I was old enough to have memories so I really don't recall all that much about their lives. There were a few stories passed down from my older siblings and my parents that I remember and some events that I witnessed first hand.

My maternal grandmother was a redhead and she passed that trait down through her genes to each generation. One of her children, my uncle, was a redhead as I am (or was when I had hair) and I have a nephew who is a redhead, a niece, a grand niece and one of my daughters have inherited the trait also. My grandmother was born very poor in 1864 in a place called Soreditch in Middlesex County at the edge of London, England. The area is now Leytonstone. When we translate old English to our Modern En-

My maternal grandmother, about year 1890

glish, we find that the name Soreditch translates to *sewer ditch* telling us that it most probably was not the best district in town. In my vivid imagination I can visualize it and even almost smell it. Today, we have a saying about being born on the "wrong side of the tracks". Think what it may have been like to have perhaps been born on the wrong side of the *"sewer ditch"*.

My maternal grandfather was probably born somewhere in Eastern Canada. I know little about his beginnings. His path led him to meet and marry my grandmother in San Francisco, California in 1849. His trip to the west must have been a long one and difficult for sure. Somehow, he passed through Illinois and Kentucky or Tennessee on his way west. It was in Kentucky or Tennessee that he was purported to become interested in racehorses, which led to his dream of raising racehorses on his mountaintop homestead.

My grandmother's trip from England was certainly not an easy one. Her poor family raised enough money somehow to buy passage for her to America where it was supposed that she would become rich. After all, America was then considered to be the "promised land", "*the land of milk and honey*". No one could have ever imagined the profound hardships that she would be forced to endure. She had passage in steerage, down in the hold of a steamship to New York and then on to San Francisco by rail. Transportation

My maternal grandparents and son posing for a wedding picture

by train must have seemed like pure luxury to her after a month or more in steerage on a steamship. Steerage was the cheapest of all fares. It was down in the hold where they hauled cattle in one direction with people as the cargo on the return trip. We can suppose that some people may have died on the voyage and we know for certain that most everyone would have been seasick for at least part of the trip if not for its entirety. Think of it, no air conditioning, no windows or portholes, no plumbing. Imagine for a moment, the smell of the vomit, the body odor, the urine and the excrement. That trip was not anything like the cruise vacation of today, I tell you for sure.

Somewhere along his way westward, my grandfather met and married a woman and they had a child. I don't know the details, but it came to pass that he was single again; this time he was both a bachelor and a father. He needed a nanny to help with the care of his son so he ran an ad in a San Francisco newspaper. "*Nanny Wanted*" was the content of the ad and this poor, young, redheaded girl all alone seven thousand miles from home responded. More than likely homesick and most likely very hungry, she was at last going to have a paying job in America, the "*land of milk and honey*".

This is how they met, my maternal grandfather and grandmother. It was considered sinful in those days for a man and a woman to even live in the same house unmarried. I doubt very much if falling in love was even considered. Love would have been an unaffordable luxury, practicality was the overwhelming necessity. They were married in San Francisco.

It is plain to see that the young redheaded girl had now jumped out of the frying pan and into the fire. She had traded her life by the *Sewer Ditch* for a life in a one-room cabin with a dirt floor and no running water on top of a mountain near Scotia, California.

My grandfather riding his bull

Think of it, this cabin was just post-and-beam, board-and-bat all hand split from redwood logs with hand split redwood shakes for a roof. If you have ever been inside of an old barn where you can see daylight through the single walls and roofs, just imagine what it would be to live in one of those kind of buildings. It had nothing of our modern construction, no floor, no insulation, no luxuries of any kind, just a simple bed and a cook stove. This was the life of the earliest pioneers and my mother as she grew up.

My grandfather worked as a *"bullwhacker"* for a time. A bullwhacker is a bull team driver. Teams of bulls were used to drag enormous redwood logs through forests to be loaded onto trains or sent in the river downstream to the mill. The bullwhacker was the man behind the whip and goad used on those unpredictable bulls. No doubt he was good at his craft but eventually, all bullwhackers were forced out of work with the advent of steam logging. After that he was forced to work as a bull cook around the various logging camps then in operation. They were inglorious jobs, carrying and hand-pumping water and carrying garbage out to the hogs that were always kept near the camps for butchering for fresh meat.

My grandfather never owned an automobile and he was often seen riding around on his bull when almost everyone else had a horse. He was considered an oddball in his later years but it is my guess that he was just from another time, another place and a different era. Most likely misunderstood, he was just a relic from the past as we all come to be.

It is easy to understand how my mother's future and character were shaped when you consider where, and who, she came from.

Chapter 3

Paternal Grandfather and Grandmother

My grandfather, George Evans, knew a different time, a different world. Born in 1842, deceased in 1895, thirty-seven years before I was born. I knew little or nothing about him until my wife and daughters, who were interested in family history, began their research. I can remember my father saying that his parents died leaving him an orphan at an early age. His mother had died when he was eight years old and his father died when he was about twelve. I can remember my father saying that he had lived in a mining town called Ruby City, Washington Territory which is now called Washington State. That is all I ever knew about my paternal grandparents. It could be that my father never talked about them, but more likely, I didn't listen as is typical of young people. It was the research that my wife did on my grandparents that brought them to life for me many years after their death.

Grandfather George was born in Maine in 1842. He had a *"good common school"* education according to a statement in his obituary.

His life was hard and tough, filled with hardships of a sort we can hardly imagine today. The records show that he was paid a bounty to join the army as was the custom in those days. He was paid $35.00 to fight in our Civil War, one of the most horrendous and bloodiest wars ever fought on the earth and certainly the most costly to be paid for in the human lives lost for the United States of America. The records show that he was wounded by a rifle bullet to the shoulder in this war and was captured and taken prisoner by the Southern army not just once but twice. He was held captive where he suffered unimaginable agonies in an almost indescribable prison hell hole.

After his discharge from the army, he left Maine. We don't know why he left, perhaps jobs were difficult to find or perhaps he was just feeling the need for adventure, answering the call to *"go west"* as was the case for so many of those frontiersmen in those days. We don't know how he traveled to the west coast of the US. He could have walked all the way. It would be a long, hard 3,500 miles but in those days, that kind of trek wasn't at all uncommon. He may have ridden a horse all the way or he could have even taken a train at least part of the way. The most likely mode for him to travel was job-to-job, working his way west on foot or horseback or even by rail, just a hundred miles or so at a time.

The next record of grandfather George after the Civil War was when he passed through the state of Michigan and later was living in Anderson Valley, California near the Pacific Coast in Mendocino County. It was in Anderson Valley that he married my grandmother Mary, the eldest daughter of John Gschwend, an early pioneer in the valley.

Life must have been very hard for this young couple. George worked for a time for his father-in-law building a toll road from

My paternal grandfather,
(no picture of my paternal grandmother is known to exist)

the town of Booneville across the coastal mountains east to the town of Ukiah some 20 miles or so. Later, according to his obituary, he worked in partnership with his father-in-law (my great-grandfather) in a lumber mill. Hard luck struck once again when the mill burned to the ground and all was lost.

Once again George was on the road. Now he had a wife and a young family. Some of the local people, years later said that they thought that they might have gone to southern California. At this time, we have no idea for sure where they may have gone, perhaps they went to the Santa Cruz area, a small town, just a few miles south of San Francisco. There was logging and sawmilling in the area and this type of work is what my grandfather was accustomed to. Records show that a George Evans had filed a claim for a 160-acre parcel of land around that time but it doesn't name a wife or children so there is no way to know for sure if it was my grandfather. Both George and Evans were such common names that it could have been someone else.

It was in Pendleton, Oregon that their trail was next found. It was nine years after the family left Anderson Valley. We don't know what kind of victories they may have encountered or hardships for that matter, but we know that even the best of times would have been hard according to our standards today. My father had been born in 1883, the seventh of ultimately eight children in the family. He was born in Umatilla, Oregon not very far from Pendelton. A deed was found in the Umatilla County Courthouse and documented the purchase of 160 acres of land. The property was about ten miles out of town. Looking at it today you would find it is prime wheat land with no buildings of any kind, very dry land where water would be very hard to find. It is prime wheat growing land today but even so I'm quite sure that it was just sagebrush and rabbitbrush when my grandfather filed his claim. He sold the property not once but twice. He repossessed it after it was sold the first time after a little while for non-payment according to contract.

The family trail was next found in a census. It showed that they had moved downstream about 90 miles to the small town of Cleveland, Washington on the opposite side of the Columbia River.

By this time, 1885-1886, they had already covered at least 700 miles since they had left Anderson Valley, and this all by wagon, by horseback and on foot. We can assume that life was very hard. We can speculate that they camped a lot in a covered wagon and that they lived in simple cabins sometimes found abandoned by squatters and fortune seekers who traveled before them. They may have lived in cabins furnished by the farmers and ranchers they may have worked for. It's reasonable to assume that they had never known the pleasures that we so take for granted today.

It was in 1888 that they arrived in Ruby City in what is now Washington State. It was a mining town about 12 miles south of the Canadian border, a boomtown, gold and silver were the quest of the miners. Those early pioneers thought that it was going to be a paradise. The town was typical *boom and bust*. In the beginning, it was just a wilderness. In only nine years, it became a boom town of about 1200 people declining in about three years next to nothing, a ghost town, a relic of better days. Some of the wooden building's lumber salvaged by ranchers and the rest disappearing in the flames of the first forest fire that passed through.

According to courthouse records my grandfather filed two mining claims, the *Baltic and Niagara* claims. We found no evidence that he actually mined any ore at either one but it appeared that someone else did, (new owners at a later date). He and grandmother Mary also bought two lots in the town. The county sheriff bought milk from my grandmother leading to the speculation that they must have had a cow and the milk was probably bought for use by prisoners in the jail. It's amazing to me how much information can be found in those old courthouse records.

My grandfather worked as a road supervisor in a nearby district for the county and as a contractor, he built a bridge across Salmon Creek for the sum of $100.00 He later assumed a mortgage in partnership with a man by the name of F. G. Woods for a saloon.

The family was now over 1,000 *horse-and-wagon* miles from their beginnings in Anderson Valley and once again faced with hardships that we can only imagine. George applied for a Civil War pension at Ruby City and just a few months later, arrived back in Anderson Valley with just three children. The older children had all gone off to find their own miseries and he had lost two of the younger girls to disease in one 24-hour period. It was a long time in research before my wife found that my grandmother Mary had died and was buried at Ruby City. Her grave would have been a simple one, just a few spades full of dirt and a wooden marker which would have burned to ashes the first time there had been a forest fire. We assumed for quite awhile that she may have died on the wagon road back to California. This would not have been at all unusual considering the hardships of a thousand mile horse and wagon trip. My father was one of the children to arrive back in Anderson Valley with my grandfather. My grandfather was soon to lose another daughter before he came to peace and rest at his passing in 1895.

You can see from this story what kind of characters my grandparents must have been. They would have been tough, they would have been courageous, they would have been enterprising, resourceful and hard-working. They would have to fight and struggle for the simplest of pleasures that we all take so for granted today. They were the essence of the pioneer frontiersmen and women who helped make America great.

Chapter 4

Mother

My mother was a character. She had grown up, the eldest of twelve
children to about age 12 on a mountaintop homestead in a cabin
with a dirt floor. She had known and felt the pangs of desperate
hunger and she knew what it was like to live without modern
comforts. She would carry all the water the family would use up to
the cabin from the only water source, a spring, many yards from the
house. They didn't need many cupboards in the cabin; there were
no trees to provide fruit, or vegetables of any great quantity from
the poor mountain soil and no river nearby to provide fish. The
only transportation was by horse or mule or "*shanks mare*" (on foot)
through mountain trails to the valley below nearly 12 miles away.
She would not have even been allowed to go to school if not for
the generosity of a family friend in the valley below who insisted
and convinced my grandfather that she should be allowed to stay
with the friend's family so she could attend a small school nearby.
My grandfather, a rather odd character himself, had filed a homestead claim of 320 acres on the mountaintop with the idea that he

An example of my mother's hand-writing at age 75

would breed and rear race horses. Not having any schooling himself, he saw little reason for a young girl to get an education. It was only because the friend insisted and prevailed with my grandfather that my mother was allowed to stay down in the valley and go to school. She had a late start, but still she graduated with honors at the age of 14 from the eighth grade and her penmanship was an exercise in perfection almost until her death at age 94. It was evidence of the effort she put into her success in school. She always felt education was important. She knew it was a sacrifice for herself and for her family and because it came with a price, it was all the more precious to her.

At the age of 16 she worked in a logging camp waiting tables and as a "salad cook". It was there that she met my father and married at age 18.

With the lifestyle that my mother was accustomed to in her early years, it is easy to see that her character would be molded far differently from ours. The privations of her early life shaped her character and surfaced throughout her life as attitudes of frugality and prudence.

One of her fundamental beliefs about life was the old slogan "*Waste not, want not*" and she practiced that premise always. Because of her beliefs, even though we were a large family of ten kids, we never went hungry. She always planned at least a year into the future. She planted, she harvested, she preserved the food, planted fruit trees for the future and like a squirrel, stored every bit and morsel of food whenever she could. She planted strawberries, blackberries, raspberries and loganberries, and then she picked them and preserved them. With the help of the kids she picked wild strawberries in the early spring followed by wild blackberries and later in the fall, wild huckleberries, (there wasn't a berry bush that was safe from picking within miles). There were wild hazelnuts to harvest too along with the walnuts from the four large trees that she and my father had planted when they first acquired the property. She would sell these nuts to ready customers and use the profit from the sale to pay the property taxes. Each year, the harvest grew at the same rate that property taxes increased. The undersized and blemished nuts were stored and consumed by the growing family.

Yes, my mother was a character for sure. She worked long and hard to impart morals and old-fashioned values to all ten of us kids. She must have been good at it too judging by the results. All ten of us became hard-working. None ended up in jail and not one of my nine sibling's families were split by divorce or dependent on others for their living.

She had a lot of old-fashioned philosophies and some interesting sayings to live by too. I wish I could remember them all. When I was young and the older siblings would start *ragging* me about being *"slow-witted"* and shy, my mother would say, "Still water runs deep", (she was really giving me the benefit of the doubt with that one). You've all seen those signs along the road that say "Slow, Children". Well, if our family had lived along the country road instead of at the end of it, there would have been a sign out front that read

"Slow, Child"! When my siblings wondered whether I would ever have brains enough to get anywhere as an adult she would say, *"You can't tell how far a frog is going to hop by the size of his warts"*. And finally, when still unmarried at thirty years old, my siblings would tease me about not finding a mate, my mother would say, *"Somewhere there's a lid for every pot"*.

A hard-working woman, my mother had little time for foolishness. She had learned early in life that food and other necessities didn't come easy and sometimes not at all. She cooked, she preserved the bounty of the land, she baked bread and she kept the house warm by coaxing heat out of that old wood-fired kitchen stove and the wood heater in the living room. She sewed and mended clothes on the foot-treadle sewing machine and she mended socks by hand. She washed piles of laundry from our large family, at first by hand with a washboard and tub and various other contraptions and later, when my folks could afford it, they acquired a used Maytag

"Home sweet home"

washer with a gasoline-powered engine. It was a *wringer-type* washer that squeezed most of the water out of the clothes as she ran each garment through one at a time. It wasn't entirely safe to operate either. If it caught hold of your fingers, it was entirely possible to peel the skin off of your arm clean up to your ears. She never had the luxury of an electric clothes dryer but rather hung all the clothes on a long line out back. It was the custom in these early days to do all the clothes washing on Mondays and it was an all day job. Every Monday, clothes would appear on all the clothes lines as if by magic, but it wasn't magic at all, just a tremendous amount of hard, back-breaking work. There were diapers hanging on the line, there were pants, shirts, dresses, long underwear and various *"crotch covers"* that they called *"unmentionables"* in those days and occasionally a pair of boots that had been washed out and hung up to drain and dry.

If the weather happened to be wet and stormy, all this stuff was hung all over the house and on the backs of chairs usually as close to the cook stove and living room heater as possible.

My mother didn't do all this work alone of course. The kids had to help. The youngest would get the easiest jobs but as they got older, the jobs would get harder until they would be as difficult as what my mother was doing. This was how the girls learned to do the household jobs that they, in their turn, would have to do when they themselves became mothers. This is how they learned that if life was going to be that *"bowl of cherries"*; it was going to be a hell of a struggle to get there.

Dishes, think of those dishes that had to be washed each day. No electric dishwasher in those days, just a lot of elbow grease with water sometimes hot and sometimes not. Early on, before my de-but into the family as number 9 of 10, water had to be carried from the spring. Later, as I grew up, we had a well and a windmill with a big water tank on stilts about 20 feet high that provided water by gravity to the house and barn. This was certainly a big improvement over what some of my older sisters and brothers had to deal with. However, the wind didn't always blow and the water didn't always flow so sometimes the water still had to be carried from the spring. I think this may have been what David was writing about in his Psalm in the Bible, which states, "*He leadeth me beside the still waters*". We hear this Psalm today mostly at funeral services. Perhaps David was thinking about all those people who were working themselves to death carrying water from the spring.

My parents in their later years

Chapter 5

Father

It is easy to see how my father's character was shaped when his heritage is considered. Half-orphaned at age eight, total orphan at twelve, most likely unloved after the passing of his mother and perhaps even unlovable due to his circumstances. It was a harsh world that he came into and love as we know it was most probably a luxury that these early pioneers could not afford. Even today in our soft and pampered lives sometimes love is out of reach for some, either to receive it or to give it. Jesus Christ, some 2,000 years ago taught the world about love to a largely unheeding world and even today a few practice hate with much more fervor than the act of love.

He grew up to be tough, my father. He strove to be an honest, hard-working and just man to the world as he saw it. When he was very young, he ran away from his guardians and on horseback, made basically the same, long trek his father, mother and family made before. Perhaps he was trying to find his older brothers who had turned to mining for a living. I remember him telling me that he had gone back to Ruby City to find that it had been turned into dust and ashes. He may have wanted to visit his mother's grave. If that was so, he never mentioned it. He never found his brothers either if that was his goal and I doubt if he found his mother's grave, after all, about nine years had passed and the fires and ravages of time had taken their toll. No doubt he just stopped for a few minutes, sitting in his saddle with his memories of his mother's love that she had bestowed upon him. Perhaps he just sat on a large rock under a pine tree and remembered his mother's laughter in happier times. When all else is gone we, everyone of us, still have our memories. I can imagine that he may have stopped his horse on the hill as he rode away from that old forlorn and abandoned townsite and turned in his saddle for one last look before heading on to his destiny.

It would be awhile before he returned to the coast of California. For the most part he worked from ranch to ranch as a cowhand and whatever else he could do for a living. He used to brag in his older years about traveling as far as where the Snake River joins the Idaho line. We speculate that he may have reached the Snake River near Ontario, Oregon. It was on horseback that he experienced the forests of pine, rimrock plateaus, sagebrush flats and verdant valleys that were his world, at the time. It was somewhere in Eastern Oregon that the urge to work his way back home must have come upon him causing him to turn westward to the Pacific Coast.

I don't know how he ever got to the redwood country where he settled into the logging camps where he met my mother, but I remember him talking about riding a cattle train at least part of the way. He said that he hired on the cattle train as a roustabout, to feed and water the cattle, he said, and for that he got free passage for himself and his horse. This would be his first ride on a steam

My father on horse-back with salmon

operated freight train and to hear him tell it, he must have thought that steam belching giant was going at least a hundred miles an hour. I could see why after riding so far in a saddle. We know that most likely, though, the train was lucky to get up to 20 to 25 miles per hour.

It was near the town of Scotia California that my father met my mother in a logging camp. Soon they were married and not too much later they had two children, my oldest brothers. They were born about a year apart in Anderson Valley where our parents moved for awhile shortly after their marriage before their return to Humboldt County. They lived in a large tent for awhile and eventually bought the 40 acres at Larabee that our family, eventually ten children in number, (and our parents), would call home.

My father was a hard man, tough and often unfair. He had

"Home sweet home" in my older siblings childhood

received some schooling but practiced little of his education. Over time I think he forgot how to read and write the little he had learned making it quite difficult to get along in this fast-modernizing world. My mother became his eyes and ears to the outside world. She would read the news to him, take care of business for him and fill out and process business papers as needed.

My father always had to have a fight going on with somebody. If there wasn't a fight, he was almost sure to start one. I think he became this way partly from his early dog-eat-dog environment and partly inherited through his genes from some of that old German stock. It is well known that some of our ancestors had always had a feud going with someone, probably for excitement if nothing else. Yes, my father was a hard man, but it is easy to see why if one just looks at the circumstances. You and I have no reason or excuse to be hard and unreasonable, but we live in a different world. There is just no way to compare our world with the past unless we consider their circumstances and their hardships.

Chapter 6

Siblings

Ours was a big family, ten kids in all, four girls and six boys. If we had been pigs, we would have been called a *litter*. If we had been pigs, we would have all had to compete for the same *nipples*. For those readers of this book who have seen a mama pig and her little ones, the last sentence would draw a picture. Mama pigs have to take care of fourteen piglets and the mama pig just doesn't always have enough nipples for everyone. Our lives were a little like the piglets as we grew up, we had to compete for space and position too, as we took our place in our large family. One thing that we should consider also, is our place in time. My oldest brother was born when his mother was just nineteen years of age, his father was twenty-nine. I had a younger brother who was born in much different circumstances. When he was born, his mother was forty-four years of age, his father fifty-four. I came along as number nine. It was an entirely different family experience for the younger children, at least in some cases, the older ones had already launched themselves out into the big wide world. The younger ones would have few if not any memories at all of the older ones being at home even if they had helped change their diapers and baby sat them while their overworked mother took care of endless chores. They can remember me as a little baby of course, but as I was a baby at the time, I have no recollection of it. The environment was quite different also for the older siblings as it was for the youngest. For the oldest, the forty acres we lived on was a wilderness. When they entered the picture space had to be made between the stumps for a vegetable garden and some open areas to grow grass for a cow which provided the young family their milk. There was no running water at the tap, no electricity, not even a house for shelter. The oldest children all witnessed or took part in removing stumps, digging the well, building the house, etc. By the time I entered the picture, enough land was cleared to support several cows. There was running water to the house provided by the well and windmill to a large tank from which it flowed by gravity to the house. In the beginning there was only a crude barn in which to milk the cow.

"Home sweet home" in my childhood, (it now has a coat of paint)

35

By the time I was three years old in 1935, we had electricity in the house and a new barn was being built.

One thing that was the same for all the children was that everybody worked. It may have been just a simple chore, but still you learned how to work. When you were little you brought in the kindling and maybe a little wood into the house. Maybe you would carry a small bucket of milk to the house for the next day's meals. As you got older, you got promoted. You then sawed the wood with a cross-cut saw and split it and milked and cleaned up after the cows.

It was different for the older children in other ways too. They were the pioneers on that forty acre stump ranch whereas we younger ones reaped the benefits from their hard labors. Even so, our life wasn't an easy one either. Our inheritance was a life of endless chores on a working farm. Twenty or more cows had to be fed with all the feed grown and harvested for them as well as food for ourselves. The work was endless, the chores tiresome. Like all kids, we would rather go fishing, hunting or swimming. For the older kids, the work was most likely more rewarding. They were the pioneers, the builders. They had to provide the *guts*, but at least they got the *glory*. And so it was that our personalities were shaped, by our parents, by our siblings, by our environment and by our genetic heritage of which we understand so little.

Chapter 7

Vacating the nest

I was seventeen years old when I vacated the family nest. I had quit school at sixteen and since I thought I was going to be a millionaire by the time I was 35 anyway, I saw little need for an education. Boy, did I have a lot to learn and I have been learning at least some of it the hard way ever since. The first lessons came quickly in the form of reality. It didn't take long to figure out that you worked for a living and that just a few select people inherit their riches. It didn't take very long either to figure out that other people's *income* would be my *expenses* and so it was that I entered into the workaday world. Work was never much of a problem to me though as I always enjoyed it and I've done lots of it. In fact, I still enjoy work but at 69 years of age my body is starting to protest. My body is crying out, "I've always been good to you, it's time now to be good to me." I started my young life out as a scrawny runt and it appears that I will end it the same way. An inch and a half or so I have already shrunk in stature.

As it is for everyone, leaving the nest was just the first step towards the rest of my life. Just one day at a time and one step at a time. The path that we take in our lifetime has many twists, many turns, sometimes we reach an oasis, a paradise. Just as many times we stumble into traps and pitfalls, such is the stew of life. Through it all I have had the opportunity to rub shoulders with many wonderful people and even a few *not so wonderful*. It is very hard to judge ourselves with any accuracy but it is my hope that just a few good things from my past associations may have rubbed off on me.

This all reminds me of a story a preacher told us one time. It went as follows.

A fellow was looking for a new town to settle in so when he came to town he asked the preacher, "What kind of people live in this town?" "What kind of people lived where you came from?", the preacher asked. "They were just a bunch of rats", said the visitor. "Well," the preacher replied, "you'll find that the people here are about the same." A few days passed and another man came to town looking for a place to settle. I'll ask the preacher, he thought, I'm sure he'll know what kind of people live in this town. So he also called on the preacher, "What kind of people live in this town?",

Typical sawmill in timber country in the 1950s

38

he asked. The preacher thought about this for a moment and replied, "What kind of people lived where you come from?". "Oh,
they were wonderful. I found it really hard to leave them." "That's
just about the way people are in this town", the preacher replied.
He was a wise preacher. He knew that we all find what we are
looking for in all our relationships.

Chapter 8

Sawdust and Slivers

The first major industrial job that I had was at a large sawmill, we called ourselves "*sliver pickers*". This was my first encounter with characters on the job. There was the grossly overweight, snoose-chewing guy we called "*Fats*" and a host of other colorful characters. By and large, those mill jobs tended to be monotonous as factory jobs usually are, the most exciting thing to happen all day was when the whistle blows at quitting time.

One thing I remember is that when deer hunting season approached, the excitement would build almost to a frenzy. It always opened on a Saturday and when that Friday quitting time whistle blew, "you better get out of the way or get run over", as most of those millhands headed for the hills.

I remember one old guy who had been working at the same job for about twenty years. He was an Italian from the "old country". He spoke heavily accented English and he worked on the "short end". This was on the "green chain", a moving conveyor along which about fifteen men would pull lumber off each side sorting it

Log carriage inside a mill

according to grade and stacking it for the monorail crane to pick up. The man who had the first pull, as we called it, had the best choice of lumber coming out of the mill, decreasing as it went down the green chain man by man. What finally got down to the short end could hardly be called lumber at all. Mostly it would be a few boards and slivers of wood. It was trash really, but that's where this old Italian worked. The short end was where all the new hands got their start and then they would be moved up the line according to their ability. This old Italian had been at this same job a long, long time. We wondered why. He was dedicated and a hard worker, why wouldn't he move up? Well, it turns out that the reason was security. He had security in his position and refused every offer to leave it. He knew that no one else wanted his job and his future was secure.

It only took me about six months to work my way up to the first pull. I was young and full of energy and I sort of started a contest with myself to see if I could pull more lumber than anyone

"Timber, big timber"

else and to try to beat my own record from the day before. The lumber was tallied every day so we knew exactly how many board feet we were pulling. This was otherwise a monotonous job, but I thought of the job as temporary as I honed my skills and tried every day to pull more lumber than I had the day before. If I remember correctly, my record topped out at about 32,000 board feet, almost as much as the total cut of a lot of sawmills.

It was here on the green chain that I learned that not everyone appreciates hard work. I was a mere 18-year old, (still in my *lout-hood*) working among career sawmill hands. Just a naïve kid, a kid trying to build a reputation with the boss, they thought. They didn't know that I had other fish to fry, other streams I wanted to cross. There just had to be a more exciting job somewhere, I was thinking. I thought of the job with the company as only temporary. It was here on this job that I was exposed to my first industrial jealousy, industrial pettiness. The man downstream on the green chain couldn't do anything to harm me as I had the first shot at the lumber coming out of the mill. Somehow he and the monorail crane operator got their heads together though and the crane operator started to slow down his pickup at my station. It was "*get even*" time for those guys, and at first, I didn't have a clue what was going on. There were a few grades of lumber that were compulsory to pull and if the stacks of lumber were not picked up when full I had to throw it all on the floor and pick it all up later and stack it as room became available.

It was a good tactic really, to put this young, dumb kid in his place and probably the only inspiration those sawmill lifers ever had. Eventually, I had a heart-to-heart talk with the monorail operator and things got better. He was a man about 35 years old of Portuguese descent. I questioned his *ancestry* in ways he had never heard before and from that time on we never had any trouble.

I didn't stay with the sawmill very long after that. It was time for me to move on. I had met my own challenges, which was good enough for me. I had learned some things about personalities in the workplace in the process. As time passed, I learned that those workers were just defending their turf from this new kid on the block, so to speak. They felt that I was a threat to their security. I had an unfair advantage over them really. They were stuck in their rut and my goal was to go on to other things.

Chapter 9

Logs and Timber

Only a logger would sit on a stump in an inch or two of snow eating his lunch and with a twinkle in his eye say, "What luxury!" With cold, wet feet in his saturated wool socks say, "What a paradise!" With bruises and scratches all over his aching body say "Those boys that work in town never have it this good!"

When I went to work in the woods, that's the way I found the loggers to be. If you didn't know the ways of the logger, you would wonder if they had any brains at all. They, of all people that I have worked with, share a camaraderie like no other and I think I had the most fun at work in the woods.

It was in the "big timber", where I went to work, the "tall timber". I had become a "redwood logger". It was a good time to be a logger then. It was the last part of an era. We felt like heroes in a way. We were battling and defeating the giants. The trees were big, the men were tough, no log was too big, no hillside too steep, nor mud and dust too difficult. The general public held the loggers in high regard also knowing full well that if you were going to live in wooden houses and have the use of wood products, somebody had to do the job. Not so today. Now a logger is vilified as a tree killer, a man who kills the forests just for fun so he can live in a mansion made of wood. At least that's how some of the people in the cities see the situation. Now as a former logger who has "*been there, done that*", let me tell you how it really was and still is even today. Logging is hard, tough, dirty work. Many loggers live, even though hard-working, in levels just a little above poverty in the smallest of wooden houses. They work so that they can eat. They work so that their families can be clothed and fed and so they can pay for their shelter.

Back in my father's time as a logger it was even worse as illustrated by the writings of Andrew M Prouty in his book, "*More Deadly Than War*". He was writing about the carnage of the thousands of loggers and mill-hands injured and killed in the years 1827 to 1981. Writing about a conservationist whining about the *dead trees, too many clear-cuts, erosion*, etc., he wrote the following:

"Who weeps for the thousands of men killed and crippled—these human victims—not insentient trees and rivers, but rather living, breathing men cut in two by flailing steel rigging, smashed by crumpling saws and falling limbs, crushed by rolling logs, dismembered by spinning saws? About these victims, the forest protectionists and environmentalists have nothing to say".

I believe these were men just trying to make a living the only way they knew how and everyone who used lumber were the beneficiaries.

Have you been into any city recently? Have you seen the subdivisions where people live? Have you seen the huge homes that the people are buying? The three car garages and the golf courses out back? Do all people in the cities live like that? Of course they don't but many of the people who whine about tree killers do. If you chance to see any highway or railroad near any city, you will see a steady stream of our natural resources going only in one direction, towards the city.

People in the city reap the benefits of our resources, as we all do, and then blame the country people for raping the land. It has always been this way. In ancient Hawaii, hunters killed off whole species of tropical birds so the noble men and women, the chiefs, could wear fancy feathered robes, symbols of power and majesty. Whales were almost entirely wiped out to provide oil for the lamps of the city and whalebone for the ladies corsets so that they could look beautiful in the eyes of their peers, even though their eyes were all *bugging* out from the agony. Whole species of birds were wiped out in the so-called "gay nineties" so the women of the cities of the world could strut around looking pretty with feathers in their hats. Animals were trapped by the thousands when the wearing of fur was fashionable in the cities.

Have you ever read a National Geographic story blaming the consumer instead of the trapper, logger, miner, fisherman, hunter etc. for the depletion of our natural resources? Do loggers live in huge houses? Do trappers dress their wives in furs? Do miner's wives wear fine gold? You know the answer. Let's not all be hypocrites in our thinking.

I got off-track there defending the working class. I too, see the need for conservation and environmental concerns, but it has always been a pet-peeve of mine that people, in a large part, refuse to look at the entire picture. We live in a world of abundance that others around the earth can only dream of. I, for one, think we should appreciate it.

Back to my story about the personalities of loggers. They, as a group, have the best sense of humor of any other people that I have ever worked with. Most of the ones I knew were hard-working, honest, almost all loving a good joke or a good story. If they didn't have a good story, they would make one up. If you didn't have a nickname, they would give you one. Mine was "Red" for the color of my hair. No doubt it would be "Baldy" now for the lack of it. I remember "Bergie", "Spoolie", "Pasquali", "Two Block", "Haywire", "Tarheel", and "Home Guard", just to name a few. These people were usually referred to with their nickname first followed by their first name, like "*Jack-Ass Bill*" or "*Two Drum Charlie*".

It was never difficult to recognize a logger when he was in his work clothes. In the days when I was logging we were not yet required to wear "hard hats". We thought that "hard hats" were just for "sissies" and it was with much chagrin and grumbling when we were finally forced to wear them by the various logging companies.

A black felt hat, hickory shirt with sleeves snagged, (cut off) at the elbows, "snagged jeans", (cut off well above the ankles) and high topped caulked boots was the normal costume. The younger guys would wear a belt but most everyone over thirty years old would wear suspenders. There was a good reason for the "snagged pants", as pants with a hem was a good way to take a header, sometimes the caulks from our "corkboots" as we called them, would get caught in the hem and cause a person to trip and fall on his nose.

Heavy canvas rainwear was added to the mix in bad weather. We called the rainwear "tin pants" and a "tin coat" as they became very stiff and rigid when wet and covered with mud. It was very common to just stand them in a corner to dry out at night. If they were dirty and muddy enough, they looked almost like a suit of armor leaning up against the wall.

It was very common also out in the "back country" for the loggers to just walk in to the taverns, cafes and small stores with their caulked boots on. This practice sure tore up the floors but it was tolerated and expected by the merchants and the floors were made of soft lumber just for that reason.

The loggers as a group were very colorful characters. A few were what we called tramp loggers. They considered staying at one job more than six months or so a sign of weakness. All the tramp loggers that I knew were single, migrating from one logging camp to another up and down the coastal timber country.

I didn't know it then, being a naïve kid of only nineteen years, but I realize now that quite a few of these loggers were alcoholics. Saturday night was a time to get rip-roaring drunk. They would get in fights at the least excuse to prove who was the toughest man and spend all day Sunday sobering up. They seemed to have an unwritten code of honor though, that come Monday morning, they would approach their job in sobriety. I know of only one exception to this. Only one man I knew of who would bring coffee out to the job spiked with whiskey to ease the pain of his hangover. If the boss was to find out about it, he would have been fired immediately.

There were a lot of reasons that the men needed to be sober. Logging is dangerous work. It would be very easy to lose an arm or a leg in the rigging or get crushed by a rolling log or falling tree. There were axes and saws to cut you, equipment to run over you and whipping cables that could easily slice you into pieces. Stretchers and first-aid kits were always kept handy, but the truth is, in those days, if a man got hurt bad, you could usually read about it in the *obituary column* a few days later. I think the reason in part for the loggers camaraderie may have been the fact that everyone had to look out for each other's safety. You had to look out for others and you had to look out for yourself.

I liked logging a lot better than sawmilling. Logging had more excitement, more adventure, more variety. I was very lucky in two different ways while I worked in the woods. First, I was never seriously hurt, just a broken ankle, a sprained ankle, a broken cartilage in the knee and a few serious bruises. Second, I never had to witness a man getting seriously injured or killed. Injuries and death were common enough among the men I knew, but as luck would have it, these things happened before or after my time with the various jobs. One man I knew was crushed by a falling tree just a few days after I left a job. Another man, a field mechanic, was badly burned in a fuel tank explosion and died a few days later. Another died instantly when a Cat (crawler tractor) that he was working on had a high-pressure grease explosion that went off in his face. These are things that nightmares are made of and I feel very fortunate that I was not there to witness these accidents.

Every job I worked on in the woods had at least one colorful character and sometimes more. My first job in the woods was as a "chaser". The job consisted of unhooking logs from the Cats as they came into the landing and rehooking them on the overhead rigging to load them on the truck as the "headloader" selects them. The head loader was an American-born Italian but still very "Italian" in his ways. His nickname was "Pasquali". Pasquali may have been a swear word for all I knew as I don't speak Italian, but I hope not. I think somebody told me it meant "friend". I was the new kid on the block, a greenhorn. This Italian chewed on me eight hours per day, six days per week. I learned eventually that a lot of it was in fun and as time went on, I learned that if an Italian doesn't chew on you it's probably because he doesn't like you. There were other colorful characters on my first logging job too. One of them was the "hook tender" (crew foreman). He was tall and skinny about six-foot four inches tall. He was tough though and widely known for his wildman antics when things started to go wrong. He would throw his hard-hat and yell and scream to the whole world with a vocabulary of cuss words that was unparalleled anywhere else. He loved to go into a rage just to impress the logging superintendent, questioning his ancestry as well as anybody else who may have been within hearing range. He was an actor of sorts and most of the loggers weren't bothered too much. Sometimes it was kind of fun to watch. He was skinny all right, but he was tough. I can remember one time when he got into a bar-room brawl with a burley log truck driver twice his size. The burley guy would floor the skinny guy but he couldn't keep him down. He was almost like one of those toy ten-pins that, when tipped over, would simply just pop up again. The hook tender finally just plain wore out that burley fellow and ended up whipping him real good.

There was another character in that camp too. He was an old man, I thought then, at least 65 (somehow that doesn't seem so old now). His name was Billy Hamilton. He was a grizzled runt of a man. He loved to talk me into playing, and losing, in the nightly poker games. I was the only one around who could lose twenty dollars in one night playing nickel-ante with a two-bit limit. He knew a sucker when he saw one. He sat next to me in the cookhouse dining room. I had an appetite of a nineteen-year old logger (a 7000 calorie per day appetite) which caused him some problems. One night he had enough of passing food to me. He said, "Damnit Red, I'm going to find another place to sit. I'm so damned busy passing food to you, I'm going to starve to death!"

Chapter 10

A Call to Arms

It was 1953, I was still working in the woods at the time but a nasty war was going on in Korea and Uncle Sam needed "a few good men" and a few culls too, it seems. One of my older brothers had already been drafted and served his two year term in the infantry there. He somehow survived the rigors of front-line battle and was returned home. It was in January that I got my invitation from Uncle Sam. It was just a simple request to report to Fort Ord for induction into the army. "Oh, great," I thought, "first they tried to get my brother killed. Since that didn't work, they want a chance at me." Apparently the North Korean enemy needed some more people in the U. S. Army for target practice.

It was in the army that I found out that I just wasn't the man I thought I was. I had been working in the woods full time even though I was limping a little from an earlier injured knee and broken ankle but I was nearly healed. It was during the physical examination that I found the truth. It was a culling process and I turned out to be one of the culls. My ankle injury, twisted knee and incredibly flat feet gave me a classification of 3-C. This was the bottom of the barrel as far as Uncle Sam was concerned and I was then assigned to what I was later to come to know as a *"sick-call"* outfit. It was sort of a rag-tag bunch. Those guys seemed to be suffering from every ailment known to man. We had guys that suffered the effects of polio, bad backs, club foot and almost any other ailment that you could imagine. It would be as easy to find a virgin in a whore house as it would be to find a healthy body in the whole bunch. There were probably a few imagined ailments and at least a couple of guys faking their condition but most were either healing up from earlier accidents like myself or had long-term effects from various diseases. After our induction, we were sent to Fort Lewis, Washington for our basic training.

It was in the army that I had my first real experience with other races and cultures. That part of the army was not a bad experience for me. I found that we are really all the same. We have basically the same desires, the same needs and even our opinions about the army were the same. We, most of us, just wanted to complete our two year term and go home. My best buddies were of different racial backgrounds. Two were Japanese, one each of Italian and Hispanic descent and myself, a mixture of German, English etc., the only real *mongrel* in the group. Akinaga, Aochi, Dominguez, Evans and Giuntini, an alphabetical stew it was. We had many good times together. After our first eight weeks of basic training we were allowed to have an automobile on base and dress in civilian clothes while on a weekend pass.

We had one automobile between the five of us while we were together, and we made the most of it. The army had a rule saying that we could not travel over 100 miles from base while on pass. We didn't pay attention to that. Like all other young men before us, it was our notion that rules were only made to be bent or broken. We had a lot of fun together. Money was always in short supply but we had a car and we had the enthusiasm of youth. We would pool our money together for gas or a place to stay and take off for all corners of the state of Washington. We were seeing the big wide world and exploring our universe any time that we could get a week-end pass to leave the base.

It was in the army that I learned to respect other cultures and ideals. It was there that I was to rub shoulders with other races and people of different colors. It was a good experience. I found that most all of the people I met were good people and most of the barriers between us came from misunderstandings and ignorance. As a dam in a river holds the waters back, so also are the barriers that hold back our understanding. It's only when we release the water that it can produce power for our light bulbs and water our land that grows our food. Only when it's released do we benefit. It's only when we drop the barriers between our cultures that we benefit from a bountiful mixture of ideals and ideas.

Left to right: Giuntini, Dominguez, Akinaga, Evans and Aochi circa 1953

Left to right, top row: Akinaga, Aochi, Dominguez,
Bottom row: Evans, Giuntini—47 years later, circa 2001

Akinaga, Aochi, Dominguez and Giuntini all enriched my life. Together, we were a cultural stew and we were all enriched. In just recent days, when we had a reunion, I had the pleasure of learning that they all led productive lives as I knew they would even almost 50 years ago. Since the time we were first together, we have traded our exuberant youth for wrinkles, baldness and gray whiskers but now we have memories and are much wiser. I for one, have the fondest memories of our times together.

I only spent about nine months at Fort Lewis. As luck would have it, I received orders to go to England where I rounded out my term in the army. I was indeed one of the few lucky ones who never had to experience the horrors and the miseries of the Korean War and all the suffering that went with it.

In England I found another culture. People there were more reserved, more stoic and staid than we Americans but their country is much smaller than ours. Our culture is steeped in a kind of reckless frontier style, at least for the western states. Theirs is steeped in history, much of it medieval. I drank some of that English ale in pubs that dated back to the seventeenth century. And so my character was further shaped by my contact with the British and my new army buddies from along the way. I am grateful for any of their good traits that rubbed off on me.

Chapter 11

Back to the Woods

As soon as I got out of the army I returned to logging, it was the only job that I really knew how to do and I enjoyed the work. It was normal for loggers to move around a lot from job to job and so it was for me. Sometimes a patch of timber got logged off, or the lumber market got into a slump, also the weather can lead to an unexpected layoff now and then. Frequently the supply of logs for the mills simply exceeds the demand. Oft-times the logger's itch for adventure causes him to quit his job and take one on the other side of the mountain, just for the hell of it. Such was my logging career as I returned from my hitch in the army. Logging was a job for the lower class but of all the genuine loggers I know, they just didn't "give a damn". They considered that they were in a class by themselves, inferior to no one else and a little superior in fact to those poor slobs in bondage to the daily grind, those with steady jobs obliged to the mill or factory whistle. Logging was sometimes miserable work. In winter, it was common to work knee deep in mud. In summer, the lungs were filled with choking dust. The jobs

Logging in the "redwoods"

were almost always full of risk and discomfort but in spite of all the rigors, it was never dull. Loggers considered mill workers mere robots, bound to their jobs by the mill whistle and their need for security. A genuine logger would hang his head in shame if he felt dependent to anyone. Such was a logger's life.

And this was my life for awhile after the army. This was the environment and the characters that I would associate with until 1962 at thirty years of age and still single.

There was Sven, Pasquali, José, McDougal and Fritz. These are fictitious names to protect the innocent (and the guilty) and to respect the privacy of these individuals, also to respect the dead as some of them, no doubt, have already passed on.

Sven was a Swede from the old country. He was a comical old cuss, if it was a bad day otherwise, you could almost always depend on him for a few laughs. He learned to speak English by reading as opposed to hearing which led to some hilarious versions of

English. He could mutilate the English language in such ways that if he had been an actor, he would have been a star. "*Yumpin Yimminy*", he would often say. He was a "powder monkey" (a person who used dynamite to blast stumps). He wasn't the most ambitious powder monkey and somewhat reckless, I thought, considering what misplaced and misused dynamite can accomplish. It was on a very steep hillside that I first knew Sven. He was blowing (dynamiting) stumps perhaps 800 feet or so upslope from us. He was blowing stumps to build a road for the logging trucks.

The method used to blast stumps was to set the charge as deep under the stump as possible. This was accomplished by jabbing a heavy, pointed steel bar between the roots to make a hole. It was very hard work, sometimes only gaining from 6 to 12 inches before hitting a rock or a root or soil too hard to master. Each time you got as deep as you could go, a quarter stick of dynamite was placed in this hole and set off to make it deeper and bigger. We called this a *coyote* hole. You might have to set off about 5 or 6 of these small charges to get deep enough under the stump to load the main charge. If a dynamite shot is placed under a stump deep enough and with just the right amount of dynamite, it would be safe to stand just a few yards away during blasting. Not so with Sven, when he yelled "*Fire in the hole!*", you had better find one, a hole that is, to dive into, to keep from being killed.

Well, Sven wasn't the best powder monkey in the world because he was lazy. He figured that it was a whole lot easier to place the charges shallow and make the charges big. In my minds eye I can still hear those charges going off and see pieces of stumps and roots and rocks flying sometimes 3 or 4 hundred feet over our heads and down into the canyon below.

These charges usually went off 5 or 6 stumps at a time, 20 to 40 seconds apart and it was a mad scramble to cover for us. It was time for everyone to get close behind a stump, under the bulldozer or get down low next to any other shelter you could find handy. No one ever got hurt from those flying stumps and I don't remember any of the debris ever getting dangerously close, but the threat was there. It was definitely a sobering experience.

It was a few miles away on a different job that I again had a chance to work with Sven. It was there that I was to witness the most comical thing that I had ever seen him do. He was preparing a hole for blasting under a fairly small hemlock stump while I was working only about 10 or 15 yards away. It is quite typical for hemlock trees to grow very shallow, sometimes the roots go out from the trunk like spider legs, with the bulk of the stump being almost on top of the surface of the ground.

Sven had worked his little coyote hole under the stump as deep as was needed, he figured, and it was now time to prime the hole. Priming the hole is simply a matter of using a little larger charge, perhaps a half-stick of dynamite to enlarge a cavity big enough to accept the charge, perhaps 30 or 40 sticks of powder for that size stump. These very small charges were set off with electric detonators known as "caps". They came in boxes with two wires attached to each. One end with the cap was inserted into the charge and the other end was what you attached to the detonator charger. But in this case, with such a small charge, you simply went around the back side of the stump, pulled the safety clips that grounded the wires together and touched each wire to a flashlight battery, one on top and one on the bottom This would normally be very routine. The small charge would make a little "poof" sound. The powder monkey would wait a couple of minutes for the smoke to clear out of the hole and then proceed on with the job of loading. This time it was going to be different. Sven came around the back of the stump as I stood there casually watching. He bent over real low with his back end only inches from the base of the stump and prepared to detonate the small charge. What I didn't know and Sven failed to recognize was the base of that stump had a hollow spot all covered with leaves and debris. Can you see it coming? Can you imagine for a moment the surprise when Sven touched those two wires to that battery? "*Yumpin Yimminy! Yeesus! Yeesus! Yumpin' Yimminy!*", he yelled dancing around in the smoke, fanning his rear end with his hard hat. At first I didn't know whether to laugh or cry, for all I knew, he may have been injured. Soon I realized he wasn't hurt at all except for the dirt and leaves that stung his rear end a little. His pants were still smoking from the charge. You would have to have been there to appreciate the scene but I could hardly get any work done the rest of the day I was laughing so hard.

Sven was our entertainment for the most part and I think he enjoyed the attention we gave him as he butchered the English language. He was fun to be around. We would bait him to say words we knew he couldn't pronounce, then laugh at his attempts. He was a comical, good-natured old geezer, we thought at the time. He was about 60 years old, (somehow that doesn't seem so old to me now) , but Sven had a dark side too as I was to later learn when I was to see him in an entirely different light. I will explain this later in the story.

"How come you didn't show up on Monday morning?", one of the fellows baited Sven. "*Vell,*" he replied, "when I *vent* out to catch the bus, I found out that they had changed their *skeh-diddle* (he was drunk) so I went back into the bar and somebody gave me a "*Mike-ee Finn*" (a spiked drink)", Translation, (he got even more drunk), he added. This guy kept us laughing all the time with his antics and his broken speech. He had missed his calling, he should have been a comedian. A refrigerator was a "*ref-rig-a-tor*" or "*sir-wel*", "Servel" gas refrigerators were a common brand name at the time. "Frigidaire" was also a common brand name leading him to oft-times call refrigerators "*frig-ee-dearies*". Where most Swedes I had known were tall, strong men, Sven must have come from different stock. He was a real small, grizzled-up old runt. Really it would take about one and one-half of him to be as big as the average Swede I had known. When asked why he was suckered into taking a Mikey Finn he would say that he was just caught "*yew-na-vares*". He would say that he "*kuh-nocked and kuh-nocked*" on the door and "*no vun vood*" answer. When the bugs were flying in the summer, he would say that the "*guh-nats*" were driving him crazy. When he spoke of the Disney character "Mickey Mouse", he pronounced it "*Mike- ee Mouse*". When he went on a toot on New Years Eve, he simply said that he had drank too much "*sham-pag-nee*".

It was later, as his cabin partner, that I was to learn more about Sven. We shared an old saw-filing shack out in the woods near the job. The owner of the logging outfit was glad to have us there rent-free as a deterrent to vandalism of his logging equipment. It was a dry cabin (no running water). It was crude, but it kept out the rain. We each had a small bed to sleep on, empty dynamite boxes for furniture, a butane gas cooking range and a gas refrigerator to round out the furnishings. Except for the lack of running water, we were in the lap of luxury as far as we were concerned. We had running water nearby in a cold, very cold, mountain stream. Have you ever had to take a bath in a cold mountain stream? It's tolerable in July and August but the rest of the year the decision would have to be made whether you would brave that cold water for a bath, bathe at the sink (also with cold water) or stink. Many times we chose the latter, I assure you.

Sven's job was to do the cooking in this arrangement. He said he could cook and as I could barely boil water, I thought it to be a good idea. My job was to do any cleaning and the dishes. I began to wonder if it was a good choice though when one day Sven brought home a "capizoni" which he had bought from a commercial fisherman, (I'm quite sure that this spelling is wrong but I couldn't find it in the dictionary). A capizoni is a salt water fish that he had purchased at the dock. A capizoni has a huge head with whiskers, looking very much like and even uglier than a catfish, even a "bullhead" looks better than a capizoni. This one was about 16 inches long and weighed about 5 pounds. This was the ugliest fish I had ever seen. I could barely look at the thing and now I couldn't believe that Sven expected me to eat it. I'll get through it somehow, I thought, maybe I can eat it with my eyes closed. I was in for another surprise. The first thing Sven prepared was the fish head. You can imagine my surprise to walk up and stare down into that pot and see that ugly brown fish head staring back at me with a rather lop-sided toothless grin, its bulging eyeballs staring back at me like the dead fish it was. "You've never eaten anything really good until you've eaten fishhead stew", Sven said as he poured on the salt, herbs and spices, "*Ya*, it's *wary* good", "*Yumpin Yiminy*". "I'll never be able to close my eyes tight enough to eat any of that thing", I said. I was really having a hard time just to keep from gagging up my lunch. The next big surprise I got, was to see that the first thing Sven ate was the eyeballs. "*Yumpin' Yimminy*! "This is food for the gods", he said, smacking his lips in pleasure. I found something else to eat, alone, as the sight was hard to witness.

Sven had another peculiarity that we laughed about. Due to the work loggers do on steep hillsides, it is common that loggers are prone to muscle cramps, especially leg cramps. They would usually come at night. They were very painful and they would bring you up out of bed in a hurry, fighting for any position that might bring relief.

Imagine my surprise to hear Sven roaring up out of bed in the middle of the night. *"Yeesus, Yeesus! Yumpin 'Yimminy!* This hurts like hell!"*, he would say. He would stumble through the darkness to the door and on outside. When he finally came back in I asked him if he was feeling okay. *"Oh ya,"* he said, "I just *vent* outside to put my foot on the ax." Further he explained, "If you have leg cramps, the best cure is to put your foot on a cold ax." *"Ya,"* he said, "it *verks* every time". After seeing this spectacle a few times, I asked him why he didn't bring the ax in by his bed. "Too *varm* in here," he replied, "have to keep it outside *vare* it's cold, *ya*, it *verk* everytime."

Sven was a real character and a lot of fun to be around but he did indeed have a dark side. I was soon to learn that he was a full blown alcoholic. He could avoid alcohol and stay on the job for a month or even a few months and then go on a rip-roaring drunk. Sven didn't have a car, he always got someone to take him to town as needed. The first few times he told me he wanted to go to town, I cheerfully offered to take him. I was totally unaware of the hell I was to suffer later.

Whiskey was what he went to town for and upon our return he got rip-roaring drunk. When he couldn't work the next day, he told everyone that he had the flu and couldn't work for a few days. I am still amazed at how many people he could con into bringing him booze. At first it was hard whiskey, but eventually, it came as cheap wine and by the case. He would even pour a cup of coffee half full and top it off with cheap red wine. By this time, for him, booze was his lifeline, for me it was hell.

Where at first, I was his friend, now that I wouldn't cooperate with going to town after booze for him, I had become his number one enemy. I worked hard all day. I had to sleep at night. He slept a lot during the day and as a result, he would stumble and mumble around in various stages of drunken stupor for most of the night. Life was getting hard for me. It was hard to get enough rest. One night it all came to a head.

It was hard enough to live with him as it was, but one night, he pulled a pistol out from under his bed and waved it around drunkenly. He threatened to show me that he had the equalizer. He was just drunk and I don't think his intentions were to shoot me, but with that kind of a threat hanging over your head, you're not going to sleep very sound, if at all. Even without the pistol, the ax and a few other tools around could do a pretty good number on your body while you're asleep if he had bad intentions as I so fearfully imagined.

I had been telling my fellow loggers at work how bad it was, how it was beginning to wear me down. If I had been older and wiser, I would have just packed up and left the cabin at the first indication of trouble. As it turned out, it was my older, wiser boss who saved the day. He knew I was at the end of my rope. The eviction was easy for the boss it turned out. He just promised Sven that he would take him to town to get some booze and left him in a cheap skid-row hotel.

I never saw Sven again, in fact, the next thing I was to know about him appeared as an article in the newspaper. He had been living as a caretaker at a duck hunter's cabin on a small island in Humboldt bay. The article said he had drowned. Someone had seen him fall out of his row boat and, by the time they could get to him, it was too late. Was he drunk?, I wondered. Did he fall out of the boat in a drunken state and was he just too drunk to climb back in? I never learned the answers to my questions.

Sven wasn't a bad man. He was a lot of fun to be with, when he was sober. He had a special personality that made us laugh. He was a very comical Swede. Sven was just the product of his background as we all are. His personality resulted from the genes that were passed down to him. He was a victim, if you will, of his circumstances.

Pasquali wasn't as colorful as Sven but he was still a notable character. He would rant and rave in his Italian way, chewing on anyone who would listen and put up with it. *"Mama Mia"* he would say to emphasize any point he wanted to make. Some of the men didn't like some of his antics, but I thought it was kind of fun. He was hardly an Italian at all, being American born. He mostly just pretended to be this persona he had chosen. He was Italian though in all ways that were visible.

Jose was from Mexico. You could tell he was of Castillian Spanish descent by his very black hair and pale skin. He had come to America a couple of times illegally and was sent back by immigration. When I knew him, he had imigrated legally and was working hard to send money home to relatives and his wife. He would work about eight months with us and then return home to Mexico to spend the winter. He was very intelligent and serious-minded. We were horsing around and playing jokes on each other most of the time which I think he thought was rather silly.

A friend and I went down to Mexico to visit him one winter. He lived in a very beautiful area near the central west coast of Mexico. Large pine trees covered the mountains in that area and in the valley, sugar cane and other crops grew on the farms.

He and his wife lived in a very simple adobe house, but even so, he was somewhat of an aristocrat among his family and peers. He owned some buses that he hired out to transport farm workers. He also had some large flat-bed trucks for hauling farm goods which he would rent for hire. He hired relatives to operate the equipment while he oversaw the operation. It appeared that he was doing very well both socially and financially.

McDougal was just a little older than I was when we first went to work in the woods. He was a good worker, much more serious than I was, more career-minded and smarter than I was too. While I was bouncing around from job to job, he stayed put working for the same company and eventually became a logging superintendent. I don't believe he was ever drafted into the army, which may have helped his career a little but mostly I think it was his serious approach to work that led him to advancement. Our paths never crossed again after that first year or two of work, but I had heard from others that he had done very well as a career logger.

Fritz was a German as you have probably already guessed from the sound of his name. He had a heavy German accent when he

Fritz on the left and "dat nutty hooker" on the right.

spoke. He was getting old, already all *gray around the muzzle like a "grizzled-up old dog"*. Like an old dog too, his feet hurt when he walked. His knees were bad. He was all stove up, as the loggers used to call his problem. He was tough but he was just getting too old for the work.

Fritz too had a problem, which was a demon for him, he just couldn't handle alcohol. Oh, he had a lot of practice all right, and when he was on a spree, he would drink enough that would probably kill any other man. He would go a month or two or three and never touch a drop of liquor. Then he would go into town and stay drunk for a week. When working he would usually stay in some little shack near the job if he could find one, usually not much better than buildings that we would use to house goats. He would take the proceeds of just one payday and stretch it out for weeks on just a few essentials while he was camping in his shack with just a camp stove, lantern and two or three blankets for comfort. When he finally would get to town, the first thing he would do was cash all those pay-checks that he had been squirreling away and go on a big drunk. It would be a week or two before we would see him again. He'd come back sickly-looking and hollow-eyed, healing up from his hangover and now he was finally ready to go back to work. "What happened to all of your money?", we would ask, "*I spent it on all those dancing girls*", he would reply.

It was at just one of those little shacks that Fritz was living in, where one of the funniest things happened. The shack he was staying in was only about 8 x 10 feet in size and it had neither heat for warmth nor a bed. Fritz had nailed up a few boards for a bunk on which he placed a few blankets and a few more boards in the corner for a table. For him, this was home, his summer palace. "How is it going today, Fritz?", we would ask. "*Ja, I'm living in the lap of luxury*", he would reply in his heavy German accent.

He had a camp stove and a few utensils for cooking and a kerosene oil lantern for reading at night. The camp stove and the few utensils sat on the little corner table he had built. It was his kitchen actually. Since kerosene oil lanterns always smell bad after they are extinguished, for convenience, it was always placed on a small stump outside when not in use. A small lean-to outhouse stood out back to complete the comforts.

This was the very scene that our hook tender (job foreman) walked up to one Sunday morning. This hook tender was quite a character himself, best known for his hard-drinking lifestyle and crazy off-the-wall stunts. On this particularly nice, sunny Sunday morning our hooker, as we called him, was on a sort of mission. He was wanting to have some fun. He was carrying something in a large bag and for some target practice, he had a 22 caliper automatic pistol as well.

The hooker had been looking for something for target practice and there it sat, the kerosene lantern sitting securely in its usual place on the stump. You can visualize the rest. After about nine shots out of that automatic, that poor innocent lantern was shot to bits. Its glass was shattered, its fuel tank full of holes and its kerosene pouring out like blood from a wounded animal.

The hooker had good intentions really. He had brought along a better lantern in his bag. It was a much better lantern in fact, a gas lantern. It would be much better for reading and it wouldn't smell so bad. He just couldn't bear to give it to Fritz without a little fanfare and fun. Fritz didn't think this whole thing was very funny at first but when questioned about it later, he replied, "*Ja, I taught dat hooker had vent crazy, he is one nutty hooker for sure*".

It was while working with Fritz that I experienced what every logger dreads, a logging accident. Every logger knows in the back of his mind that an accident can happen at any time. The laughing and playing, the good-natured horseplay and all the rest, was a kind of screen in a way, to cover and protect his feelings and fear from his environment. Logging just as all other industries, has become much safer over the years, but for those old-time loggers, great risk was a way of life.

We were logging on an "easy show" as the loggers called it. The ground was good, not very rough, and the timber lay thick on the ground. We were logging with a set of wheels. That's what they called an arch that was pulled behind a bulldozer. If you've never seen a logging arch, think of it as a hoist to lift the front of the logs off the ground for towing which allows the dozer to pull a larger load. The dozer would tow this contraption like a trailer, itself on its own set of tracks. A cable would run up the boom and over the fairlead (roller) from the winch on the dozer and a butthook was attached to the end of it. The arch really consisted of only four major parts, the boom which arched up like the tail on a squirrel

Logging arch

Bulldozer with arch pulling redwood log

with the fair lead on the end about twelve feet off the ground, a u-shaped horizontal frame and its two sets of tracks.

We had set the chokers on the logs and we were going to hook the chokers on to the butthook and were preparing to proceed. The cat and arch themselves were on pretty good ground but the logs laying very steeply endways uphill. They were small logs, about three feet in diameter. We didn't think of them as threatening in any way. Neither of us had even the slightest clue that there was any danger. I was giving hand signals to the cat operator to back the arch sharply up the hill to Fritz and myself for the intended hook up.

By this time, we were already straddled by the tracks and the u-shaped frame of the arch and I was giving the dozer operator the signal to stop. That's when it all began to happen. The vibration of the dozer was enough to shake one of the logs loose from its bed behind us and it started to move. It began to slide right down into the u-shaped enclosure the arch created. It was a kind of trap really, that we had unknowingly set for ourselves, and there was little time for escape. I was a young man then and with all the strength I could muster, I jumped up and over the u-frame to safety. It's amazing how far you can jump when your life is at stake. For Fritz, it wasn't so easy. He was stove up with age and he knew that his only option for escape was to drop down and go under that u-frame. Fritz just ran out of time. He managed to move to the side of the frame which was to save his life. The end of the log slipped on past him and came to rest at the deepest part of the frame. If Fritz had gone there, he would have been crushed like a fly under a fly-swatter. Fritz was by now in an awful fix. He was caught between the frame and the log right at chest level. He was now facing the log. It seemed to me that his eyes were *bugging* out like a mouse in a mouse-trap and he was turning blue because he couldn't breathe. This was a terrifying experience for me. I knew that if we didn't get Fritz out of that predicament real soon, he was going to suffocate, not to mention any injuries that may have already occurred. The situation was critical, something had to be done immediately or I was about to witness a man die right in front of me. Fortunately, loggers use hand signals for almost all communication with each other. With a flurry of hand signals, I directed the dozer operator to move ahead slowly thinking that we could gain a little more space for the injured man. This seemed to make matters worse, as the arch moved forward, the log simply slid forward with it. We were really desperate now. There seemed to be only two options, pivot the arch to the left and create a space for Fritz or run to get help from another dozer. It would take at least twenty minutes to get another dozer into position to roll the log away from the man's chest so that was a last resort. In twenty minutes, Fritz would most likely die from suffocation. We had no choice, we had to try. With more frantic hand signals, we tried to move forward in a pivotal turn. We moved very slowly at first to see if our scheme was working. To our relief, the space that Fritz was in seemed to widen a little. We had more confidence now as we crept forward a few inches at a time and all at once, Fritz was free of his greatest danger, at least he was able to get his first breath of life-giving air. He just sort of slumped to the ground under the u-frame, gasping. The dozer operator and I helped to get Fritz stretched out on the ground. We didn't know how bad he was injured, but in our minds, we were sure that most every bone in his upper body was most likely broken. To our great and pleasant surprise, after just a couple of minutes, he wanted to sit up and after about five minutes, he wanted to stand up and walk almost like normal. This was all a very, very close call. It seemed as if the whole thing took place in slow motion. It took forever to get Fritz free of that awful vise that held him by the chest. It was most probably only a two or three minute ordeal, but when you are witnessing a man suffocating to death, every second is precious time. It was a few days before Fritz returned to work. It could have been much, much worse. He had some broken ribs and severe bruises, but he was a tough *old geezer*, eventually he got back to normal health.

Fritz was reaching the end of his days as a logger now, he was getting too old for such dangerous work. Logging depended on agility and speed for survival. He was well over sixty years of age by now and he was slowing down. He was getting to be all *"stove up"* as loggers called it. He was fast becoming a *"rump- sprung"* old geezer now, his *"leaper spring"* had either been broken or just plain wore out.

My experiences with Fritz all ended many years ago. I'm sure he died many years back, most likely as a lonely old man in some shack with just the memories of his younger days in the woods when he too was agile and robust. I doubt very much if he had anyone near to him that would claim his body. He would most likely just be processed as a number by the authorities. He would probably be buried in some "*marble-orchard*" all right but I doubt if there would be much of a marker of marble on his grave.

Thinking about Fritz, and Sven makes me think of my own life. I consider that I have been one of the lucky ones. I have had a life of relative ease. I have a lot of friends, a family near to me. It could have been different, a lot different and as I ponder these things, an old saying comes to mind. "*There, but for the grace of God, go I*".

Chapter 12

Construction: A New Career

It was about 1962 that I would get into a new line of work. It was in highway construction primarily as an equipment operator. It was entirely by chance that I went to work on construction. The man I had been working for in the woods had run out of timber to log and as a result was looking for work for his two bulldozers elsewhere. He had bid some jobs and as luck would have it, there was work for one of his dozers on a county highway construction job. This was a union job requiring the use of union labor. My boss requested that I be the "*catskinner*", as *dozer* operators were called and as none of the union operators wanted the job anyway, I was allowed to join. The main reason that nobody wanted the job was that it was to last only about three months, not to mention that it was too far out in the mountains.

The first requirement was the need to join the Operating Engineers union and then get hired from the "C" list for a job. It was normal for the union to call on the men from the "A" list, those who had the most seniority, first. Only when that list was exhausted would they go to the "B" list. It was usually almost impossible to get hired from the "B" list except for those jobs that came up that none of the other operators wanted. The "C" list was even worse. About the only way that you could get hired there was if a contractor specifically asked for you by name and then only if it was a kind of job that none of the "old hands" wanted.

There was a whole new bunch of people with whom I was to rub shoulders, a whole new breed. While the loggers I had known shared a very special camaraderie and always looked out for each other, these new co-workers were an entirely new *"breed of cat"*. They were much more self-centered and you had to watch your back. I don't mean to say that they were all bad, I developed many good and lasting friendships among them, it's just to say that it was a completely different group from the loggers I had known.

The three month job passed very quickly but it gave me the chance to learn a little about construction and its workers. When the job was completed, of course I then had to sign up on the union "B" list and wait for some jobs to come along that no one else wanted.

This all went along for about a year. I worked in gravel pits etc. The jobs almost always were boring and the equipment outdated, old and oft-times in disrepair. The boredom was the hardest thing to get used to. I was used to scampering around steep hillsides with new work situations every day and now I was usually confined to a very tiresome routine, just back and forth on a gravel pile.

The pay was better on construction but I was to spend many boring hours on a hot, dusty or freezing and sometimes wet dozer seat dreaming about my days as a logger. Many times I considered giving up construction and returning to the woods where the work, though less secure, was much more satisfying.

Finally I had worked through that time on the "B" list and now that I was on the "A" list, things were getting better. Now I was getting some of the better jobs with much better equipment and bigger jobs which made for a much better income. Now finally, I could pick and choose a little on the jobs where I would work. It was in 1964 that the real opportunities in construction were to come. It was a total disaster for a lot of people though.

The opportunities came in the form of a disastrous flood. It was a disaster for me also in that thirty-four acres of my forty acres of land washed down the river along with a house and other buildings.

There's nothing in the world as good for the construction industry as a big disaster. The highways were washed out, bridges were down and in this case, over one hundred miles of railroad needed to be rebuilt. At first, all of the construction equipment was put to work as a safety issue. A lot of small town's infrastructures were wiped out. Powerlines had to be replaced, sewer systems and water systems were devastated as well as routes to hospitals, etc. It was a huge disaster, it was months before the highways were open again and even more months before the railroad was to again operate. The flood was a disaster of gigantic proportions for three counties and most of its residents, but a boon for the construction industry. For most all of the contractors, the aftermath of the flood was the proverbial *"pot of gold at the end of the rainbow"*.

It was on one of those flood repair jobs that I met him. "Red" was his nickname, because of his red hair. He was a laborer. He was rather short and stout and he was smart in ways that you could not imagine. His life began in the Ozarks. He was illiterate (he could neither read nor write). Sure he would never be able to use higher math because he had no schooling, but his ability to add and subtract didn't seem to be affected very much. He would solve math problems just as you and I, I'm still baffled at his methods. I would question him sometimes about how he could work out problems in his head but he could never explain it. The process seemed to be more intuition than anything else. I couldn't understand it and I don't think he did either. He was a good man, strong as an ox and a good worker. He was an honest man without pretense, except for one thing, his illiteracy. He had learned early in life that he would be held to a lower level by his peers if his illiteracy was discovered.

It didn't take Red and I very long to form a brotherly sort of bond. He was older than I was by about ten years but we were both single men and as such, sometimes we would go to restaurants etc. together. It was at a restaurant that I first learned that he couldn't read. I thought it a little odd how he would engage the waitress in conversation. He would hold the menu and look it over just as if he was reading it, all the while asking her questions about the food, what the special was for the day, how it was prepared etc. He had practiced his little charade to perfection. He was good at it and I don't think any casual observers ever figured out that he was illiterate. Red never understood books at all but still he was smart. His world of knowledge was small but still he understood the people around him very well. His boss and fellow workers eventually figured out his handicap and immediately started to treat him with disrespect. They felt superior to him and showed it in many ways. He understood them very well, though I don't think they ever understood him. Who was the smartest among them? I wondered.

The job was a stream clearing job, a massive log jam had formed because of the flood and as a result our job was to remove it from the stream and burn it. If you were to measure the debris in tons, it would measure in the thousands. We kept a huge pile of debris burning next to that stream from the day we got there to the day we left about six weeks later.

The job itself was in a very isolated mountain area and to make matters worse, the highways were washed out and many of the bridges were destroyed. Our boss rented space for us in an old fisherman's hotel that was normally only open in the summer months and that was to become our construction camp for the duration of the job.

It was in that old ramshackle hotel that I was to witness one of the most hilarious things that I ever saw. It still makes me laugh after all these many years.

It is just normal that in burning so much debris, the workers would finish the day almost totally black from the soot and ashes. It was grimy, dirty work to say the least. It was a mad race for the showers as soon as we came into that old hotel and it was a good while before we began to feel even a little bit civilized. There were only about three showers in the whole place for the crew of about eleven guys . It was customary to wait for others awhile before you had a chance to get cleaned up.

As luck would have it, that particular day I took my turn at the showers before Red and then he took his turn. Red was really a fair haired white man but you would never have thought so this day. He was black. He was covered head to foot in black soot and ashes from the day's work. Even a native right out of Africa wouldn't have been any darker than he was. He got himself all soaped up and then it happened. The ancient water system gave up and there he was, in a shower with no water. *What am I gonna do?* he said as he appeared in the doorway. In his Ozark Mountain accent he said again, *What am I gonna do?* We couldn't help him very much, we were laughing too hard. There was Red all soaped up, a little grayer now from the lather but still almost black, a short, stout man naked as a jaybird saying "*What am I gonna do?*" he was looking like a frustrated lathered-up gorilla. It had to be one of the funniest things I ever saw.

I only saw Red a few times again after that job. I later heard that he had met and married a school teacher and that she was teaching him to read and write. Red was smart enough really. He knew more than most of us about people and it was obvious to me that he was just out of step with the times.

There were other characters in my life too and other jobs. There was a guy we nicknamed Rattlesnake and there was Mitch. Rattlesnake gained his fame by claiming he had been bitten by a rattlesnake. His rattlesnake bite turned out to be a raging hangover and he was looking for an excuse to go home because his head hurt and it was the only reason he could think of to go home early. The whole rattlesnake story became a joke with the rest of us as we knew this was not a rattlesnake area, none had ever been there before or since. Rattlesnake wasn't the only one on the crew who would drink too much and have to come up with stories to cover up the truth. Construction workers are well known to be a hard-drinking bunch as a rule therefore, a few became full blown alcoholics.

Mitch was our superintendent and he was a good one. This job was five miles of freeway through the redwood country. Mitch was in charge. It was mountainous terrain, a tremendous job with millions of dollars worth of equipment and more millions at stake for the company. Mitch could supervise a job in a manner equal to the best but Mitch was an alcoholic. When we started this particular job, Mitch was sober. He could match wits with the best of men. He surrounded himself with good foremen and the job ran as smooth as silk.

Mitch was a short, stout man with only one good eye. The blind eye looked kind of like a broken headlight on an old car. Most of the time, it just seemed to be looking for something long lost, just looking anywhere but straight ahead. He never missed a thing with his good eye as he roamed back and forth through the job. He would run the job from his pickup, with his two way radio microphone in his hand and a hard hat on his head. He seldom talked to anyone where he saw a problem but rather he would call one of his foremen on the radio to straighten it out while he would continue on to the next. His management style was a little different than most superintendents but it was effective and things ran smoothly.

It was later, about half-way through the job when things started to change. Mitch, after a long sober period, started to drink. We had a saying for that, we called it "*falling off the wagon*", and when he fell off the wagon, it affected his job in almost every aspect. I remember that one day he got so bad that he was playing *chicken* with the earthmovers. These were 100 ton machines loaded with dirt, hardly a fair contest against a pickup truck on a haul road. Fortunately for Mitch, the operators always found a way to go around him.

The foremen managed to cover for Mitch for awhile but eventually we saw him less and less and he was eventually fired by the upper management. It was time for Mitch to go home and sober up. It was time for him to get dried out.

I met a few other men in my lifetime who were very intelligent, tops in their professions too and they were alcoholics. They had spent their lives perfecting the art of hard drinking only to have alcohol master them.

There were other characters too, in my years in the construction industry who affected my life as well. Unfortunately, some sober, honest, hard-working men were not as colorful in character as the ones who seemed to have problems. "Such is life"!

Chapter 13

Marriage: A Life Changing Event

It was in 1966 that I met and married my *lifemate*. I was thirty-three years old at the time and I thought I was destined to live and die a bachelor. I was pretty sure by this time that there wasn't a woman alive who would give a hoot about me and as a defense, I had decided, "*who needs them anyway*". My attitude was that of a con-firmed bachelor. At the age of twenty, I was afraid of girls and now past thirty, the only thing that had really changed was that I had now become afraid of women.

It's never easy to explain why someone is a misfit and even more impossible to understand oneself. It seems to me though that I entered the adult world socially retarded, starting from behind in the social graces and never quite catching up. Part of it can be explained by our isolated upbringing as a family. We never attended school proms or other social functions like other teenagers. We had very little exposure or training in social circumstances. Even this, though, didn't seem to hold my siblings back as much as it did me. Somehow it just took me longer to grow up I guess.

I was awkward, easily embarrassed and bashful. I would get absolutely tongue-tied around girls. For me it was almost as if girls had not been invented yet in those days of my youth. Only those who have shared this problem could even begin to understand those inadequate feelings. By the time I reached my late twenties, most of my family and friends were beginning to worry about me. Some made attempts at match-making. They thought it was time that I should have a family of my own. Perhaps their motive was that, in their view, the time had come to plant my big feet under my own table at the Christmas, Thanksgiving and other holiday feasts. *They may have grown tired of me showing up at dinnertime with just a big appetite.*

It was my sister-in-law who introduced me to my wife. *Joy* was her name, and aptly so, living up to her name, she has brought Joy into my life, for now over thirty years.

The introduction was an ordeal for me. I felt awkward and bashful, tongue-tied and inadequate as usual, really just wishing that I was anywhere but there. It was my sister-in-law who saved the day, so to speak. She decided that she, my brother, Joy and I should all go out on the town. For my sister-in-law, the word "no" was just not a satisfactory answer. When she decided something, it usually happened..

She took the four of us out together to get acquainted. The place that she had chosen was a perfect place to get to know someone. It was a dive, a dump, a noisy, smoke-filled nightclub, but it was perfect. There was this multi-megawatt, ear-splitting speaker right over our heads blowing out honky-tonk music (noise) and it was very dark. This really helped Joy and me get acquainted. It was so dark she could barely see what I looked like (*this sure would be helpful*) I thought, and if I was to blunder in any conversation with her, it wouldn't have mattered, because the music was so loud she wouldn't be able to hear anything I said anyway. Oh, and we had to dance too. No problem at all for Joy but I had never learned to dance and now I knew that I was in "*deep doo- doo*". I was going to have to fake it. The crowded room is what saved the day. It was my lucky night. I just mostly stood there like a *dumb ox* while she just danced around having a great time. The fact that she could barely see me in the dark was going in my favor and the fact that she couldn't hear anything I said made me seem to her that I might be at least a little intelligent and debonair. It was definitely my lucky night!

Joy lived about 200 miles away from me. She was a Spanish language teacher at a small high school, a language she had learned during a seven year stay in Mexico. I never supposed that I would ever see her again. Oh, I knew I had made an impression on her all right (*the very reason I thought I would never see her again*). To my surprise, about three days later, I received a little note from her thanking me for our very short but good time together. The note had a return address on it, of course, but she had also included her phone number. Perhaps she momentarily had a lapse in good judgment I thought, or maybe she had put her phone number on the note in an absent-minded sort of way out of habit. The fact that she had left a lot of empty white space around her phone number escaped me. I just didn't understand the ways of women at all.

It was a couple of weeks before I got up enough nerve to call her, a couple of agonizing weeks. Occasionally I would have a rational thought or two. In my most rational moments, I would consider that she had three kids (that could certainly complicate things). I would think about how she had an aristocratic background and a college education , completely different from my background. My rational moments were all short-lived however. Mostly I just thought about what her perfume smelled like, *just a small dab behind each ear.* I thought about how warm her body was while we were *standing* there "dancing", *sometimes so uncomfortable yet so pleasantly close.* I was just like the proverbial lamb being led to slaughter. I was the only one who didn't have a clue what was going on. It wasn't the rational thoughts that caused me to make that call, but rather the irrational ones. The same thoughts that have brought men and women together throughout the ages. Finally, I gathered enough courage to make that call. It wasn't like she could slap me or anything. She lived too far away. *"Hello," I said, "I'm just going to happen to be in your area Saturday night and* ————————————".

It was our first date. I was so nervous that I just about cut my throat while shaving, I was still bleeding a little, in several places, in fact, when I showed up at her door. "Where would you like to go," I asked? "I don't know, where would you like to go?," she answered. I was a stranger in town, I told her, "You tell me where you would like to go." "There's a nightclub in town playing a new act that everyone's raving about," she said, "it's touted as a Las Vegas-type show. Maybe we can go there," she added. She thought, I guess, that since we had spent a few hours in a nightclub on the first night we met, perhaps this would be something that I would enjoy. I thought that she must like that kind of entertainment and since this is how we spent our first evening together, I thought it would be something that she might enjoy.

It was on this first date, in that nightclub, that we found out we had common ideas, ideals and interests. The act could only be described, even generously, as bad. The act consisted of a very tall blonde girl and two very, very short midgets. It was a comedy act and the only talent the midgets had was their ability to look short.

84

The tall blonde's talents were limited to being a tall blonde with a bust that looked like it had been pumped up with a bicycle tire pump. The script was bad. The jokes only varied a little between off color and vulgar. Neither one of us liked nightclub acts in general and nightclubs in particular. We haven't been to a nightclub in thirty-five years since that first date and if we live another thirty years, I'm quite sure that we will never go to one again.

It was a short courtship. I invested so many quarters in the local phone booth that I felt like I should own about half the phone company. Since Joy lived two hundred miles away and I was working ten hour days six days per week it was difficult to spend very much time together. We only had Saturday nights out and Sundays to get acquainted.

One day after about three months of getting acquainted with Joy (I was operating a bulldozer at the time on a highway construction job) I was anxious to see the boss. It was a beautiful summer day, it was a day when "*dirt stiffs*", as we called ourselves, were supposed to be thinking about our work. Not today, I had other things on my mind. I had been watching all day for the construction superintendent to come driving by so I could tell him something *important*. By now, it was getting late in the afternoon and I was getting anxious. Finally, just an hour or so before quitting time, he came bouncing along the rough haul road in his green pick-up truck. Now was my chance, I thought as I jumped off the dozer and hurried out to the middle of the road flagging him down.

The superintendent was a gruff individual, as most of the superintendents were. "*Waddaya want?*" he asked. "*I need two weeks off*," I replied. "*Why the hell do you need two weeks off in the middle of the summer?*" he asked. "*I need two weeks off so I can get married and go on a honeymoon.*" He looked at me with a sort of twinkle in his eye and replied, "*If you're going to go do something that stupid, I guess we can give you two weeks off.*" He was gruff all right, but he knew that if he didn't give me the time off, I would take it anyway. I just had more important things on my mind. I was thinking about that perfume, just two small dabs behind each ear.

Marriage was definitely a life-changing event for me. Joy had a lot of training to do. I was sort of like that barely housebroken puppy. Lovable perhaps in Joy's eyes, but barely civilized. One day I was single and perhaps a little reckless and the next thing I knew I was a husband and a stepfather to three boys aged 11 to 14. I had a lot to learn.

The learning started in the months following the honeymoon. There was a lot to worry about. There were financial concerns and the usual problems that all parents have raising their kids and job challenges. In my case, working in the construction industry, it was normal for me to be unemployed during the winter months. I learned a lot about women too. The first thing I learned was that if they make a statement about something of which you have not a clue, the best reply is to say simply "*Yes, Dear*". For instance, they might say, "*It's a nice day,*""*Yes, Dear.*" Or "*Did you clean out the garage like I asked you to?*""*Yes, Dear*", or "*I'm going to town to get the car washed and need $500.00,*""*Yes, Dear.*" You have to be careful though because sometimes they throw in a trick question just to keep you on your toes. They might say, "*Does this dress make me look fat?*" If you answer "*Yes, Dear*" to that one, you'll have to wade around in deep "*doo-doo*" for a week.

Women are mysterious creatures for sure, but I think they're great just the way they are. I wouldn't want Joy to change for a minute. Even though we have been married now over thirty years, I still get a thrill when she gets *uncomfortably, yet pleasantly close* or when *I smell her perfume, just a little dab behind each ear.*

There are a few things though that men will never understand about women. Why they want a house with a big picture window for instance, and then cover it up with heavy drapes so that you can't see out. Or why they want a bigger lamp for better lighting and then put a lamp shade on it so heavy that only a tiny bit of light finds its way through. Or why they scold you for not telling them about the lace on their slip showing below the hem of their dress (a real social disgrace for women) even though they wear a dress proudly with lace sewn on its hem. *Go figure!* How about when you're both going to some appointment and you wait while she talks on the phone for thirty minutes then spends another thirty minutes dressing and when you stop to let the cat out as you go to the door, she smiles at you sweetly and says, *"Honey, hurry up, you're going to make us be late."*

It's good that women are the way they are even if we men don't quite understand them. It's good that women like pretty things, soft and cuddly, warm and comfortable things. If men had their way, we would all still be living in caves. The first problem with that is that there just aren't enough really good caves to go around anymore. The second problem is that there wouldn't be any recipes for cooking and we would get sick and tired of eating the same thing every day. I can picture a prehistoric cave family sitting in their cold, dark, damp cave eating dinner. Junior speaks, *"What are we having for dinner, oh hairy daddy?"* Daddy *speaks, "Ugh, hot potato on stick."* Junior speaks, *"but I'm tired of the same old thing, oh hairy daddy."* Daddy speaks, *"Ugh, shut up, eat hot potato on stick."* Junior speaks, *"but oh hairy daddy, I was hoping for something different."* Daddy speaks, *"Here is different hot potato on stick, shut up, eat. . ."* You can see from this illustration that even our manners would leave a lot to be desired if it weren't for our women folk.

My greatest challenge immediately was to become a father to three young step-sons. We had some good times though, and in just a few short years they each in turn set out into the big wide world. James was old enough to be on his own about three years after Joy and I were married. Jon and Jeff both worked with me in the land-scaping business quite a bit and Jeff also worked for me as a land-scape foreman for a time in Alaska. I consider them all an important part of our family.

In time, our little family started to grow. First one, then another little girl was born. They were cute little things, still are in fact, though a lot bigger. I never did think that they looked a whole lot like me, but then they didn't look like the mailman, the UPS guy or the appliance repairman either so I'll just have to accept the fact that I fathered a couple of good looking kids. They were good kids too, Kathy and Susie, they brought many good and positive things into my life, I have many happy memories of our years together. They both taught me a lot about the finer and softer things of life as they are now teaching their husbands. Later on when the girls were in their mid-teens, a nine-year old grandson named Josh was added to the brood but by this time the older boys had all gone out on their own a long time past. One of them also is the father of our grandson. Time passes quickly when you're raising a family, too quickly and looking back, it seems that it was all over in a flash. First the boys went out on their own one-by-one and then the girls and finally the grandson, each in turn. Raising kids always contribute to the personalities and character of their parents. Kids bring joy, frustration, happiness, and many times much cause for worry. Life begins to get serious when you have kids, they need much comfort, food, clothing and security. They need to be loved, they need direction, they need discipline and they need to have opportunities provided. If you have not yet "grown up" yourself, that will soon change when you have children. Look at the mother robin in the springtime, she looks real pretty, every feather in just the right place all preened up for mating. Take another look at her in the fall, you'll notice that she looks all worn out and in much disarray, just about the way we look by the time our kids are able to go out on their own.

It's a lucky man who has a good mate and I consider that I am one of the lucky ones. Nothing at all shapes the character of a man in good ways more than a good woman. Nothing at all civilizes a

Picture of Kathy with then-future-husband Kevin at her college graduation

Susie at her college graduation

man more than the responsibilities of a family under the guidance and understanding of a patient woman. Nothing at all is more rewarding for a man than the love and kindness he gets from his ever-concerned wife. Why should we ever complain about them? Most likely, I think, we just get a little spoiled. Just because we now have whiskers doesn't mean we're not just still little boys at heart.

Joy has brought a lot into my life and I think I have brought a lot of good things into hers. She brought me love and understanding. She has encouraged me in everything worthwhile that I have ever tried to do. She has stood by and encouraged me just as she promised she would in our wedding vows. *What man should ask for more?* I too, have tried to bring good things into her life, just as I promised to love her and cherish her, to provide for her needs. It was a promise that I made in our wedding vows, now so many years ago. I believe that Joy has made a lot of good contributions to my personality and character. We both believe that God brought us together, knowing that we would be good for each other.

Chapter 14

New Work, New Faces

It was the year after Joy and I were married that I began to think I should find another line of work. The large good paying jobs on construction consisted of mostly highways and dams and the like. The typical job would last a year or so and then it was time to move on. This was a problem for me because I had a wife and children now and wanted a line of work with more stability and where I could be home every night. My dad had told me over and over again long ago that old adage, "a *rolling stone gathers no moss*". I could see that it was all too true. That kind of construction work was very transient for the most part. Many, if not all, of my co-workers seemed to have very little accumulated for their labors. Most of them didn't own their own homes, but rather lived in trailer parks and rental houses. Many times, an old pick-up truck, a family car and a house trailer were all they had to show for their life's work.

And so it was that I eventually found a new line of work which was to give me a host of new challenges and opportunities. It was landscaping work and the first challenge I faced was how to survive on the low pay. But the opportunities were there too; opportunities to learn new things, and rub shoulders with a whole new cast of characters and to meet a whole new set of faces.

Getting into this new line of work really was almost accidental. I was seven hundred miles from home, checking on some property that a friend and I owned in Washington State, I really had no intention of looking for a job there at the time. It was while out for a drive that I saw it, just a little sign on a fence post. "Help Wanted", it read. Maybe I should check it out, I thought, as I drove on past. A couple of blocks later I stopped and turned around to go back and have another look. I have no idea now why and no idea then why I did it. Just curiosity, I guess.

It was a landscape construction outfit and they wanted someone who knew something about machines and equipment to operate their small backhoes, loaders, etc. These were mere toys compared to the machines that I had become accustomed to, but still I thought that the work might prove to be interesting.

By the time I got into the office, I was beginning to have some second thoughts. What was this crazy thing I was doing? I was seven hundred miles from home and now the man in charge was asking me to fill out their job application, which I proceeded to do. I should have *smelled a rat*, when, without any hesitation, he said, "You're just the man we're looking for. How soon can you go to work?" Now I had to explain my situation to him. I would have to check with my wife to see if she would be interested in relocating. We then agreed that I would call him the next day with my decision.

Now I'm really in the soup, I thought as I got back on the road. My wife is going to think I've lost my mind. She had been required to move more than a dozen times in the thirteen years of her previous marriage. I had intended to bring stability to her life and now here I was preparing to ask her if she would like to move again! What could she possibly think? If she decided it was all right to move, where would we live? She had a teaching commitment at a school in California. How would we handle that? By this time, I was beginning to really get cold feet. I was beginning to wonder if the idea of relocating had any merit at all.

We had a long phone call that night, Joy and I. Much to my amazement, she saw the whole thing as an adventure. She thought a change would be good, we only had to figure out a way to make it work. It was eventually decided that since I was unemployed, I could try out the job to see if it was work that I liked to do. It was sometime in March and if the job worked out, she could move to Washington in June after she had fulfilled her teaching commitment.

The next day I called the man at the landscaping outfit as we had agreed. I explained to him that I would take the job, but first I had to go home and get my gear. All my working clothes were at home. I didn't even have work boots with me, let alone the minimal things for housekeeping. We agreed that I would go to work a week later when I returned. It was a frantic week really, to get home, settle all my affairs there and return for work. I had a lot of mixed emotions the day I left for that new adventure as I kissed my bride goodbye, *I held her a little closer and a little longer, uncomfortably yet pleasantly close, and I know that I was going to miss that perfume, even though it's just two tiny little dabs, one behind each ear...!*

It was on that first day of work that I found out how hard the work could be. The work-site was a highway rest stop. The task was to plant about sixty Douglas Fir trees. I expected to use a backhoe but they just handed me a pick and shovel. The soil was compacted extremely hard by the earthmoving machines when they contoured the site. This wasn't topsoil like you find in your garden either; but

94

instead, a mixture of rocks and roots, clay and just a little black soil mixed in. The planting holes had to be big too, three feet in diameter and one and one-half feet deep according to the job specifications. I just couldn't believe they were going to dig all those holes by hand. Machines had been invented a long time past to do that kind of work. It just didn't make any sense to me at all. A hole that was taking an hour or more of backbreaking labor to dig would only take about three minutes with a backhoe and backhoes could be rented from the rental shops for very little more per hour than the cost of a man's wages when you added in the cost of overhead.

It was a long hard day. Again, I really should have smelled a rat when they seemed so eager to hire me I thought. This was man-killing work. Useless work too, in my opinion. I would swing that heavy pick for awhile penetrating only about three inches into the hard soil, pant a little while catching my breath and then shovel the loose dirt out of the hole. Over and over again, the process would be repeated until a hole was completed according to specifications. In this kind of work you don't get a whole lot of satisfaction. When you finish digging one hole, it's just time to start another. I had hired on to operate equipment, which turned out to be a pick and shovel. I was disappointed for sure.

It was a haywire, *Mickey Mouse outfit*, but in due time, they figured out that they needed equipment and it was my job to operate it as intended. It was mostly rental equipment, small dozers, small backhoes etc. In spite of the low pay, I found that I enjoyed the work. Each day it seemed that I was meeting new faces at new places. For the most part, there were three crews working on different jobs and I moved equipment back and forth wherever it was needed most.

Chapter 15

New Job, New Challenges

After a month or so had gone by, the superintendent approached me about taking on a job as foreman on one of the crews. It wasn't something I felt comfortable with, I told him. "I don't really know very much about landscaping." I added. He answered, "We'll give you a "lead man" who knows the ropes. All you have to do is manage the job and operate any equipment that we bring to you."

And so it was that I fell into a whole new line of work. The lead man and I got along great and the work was always interesting. It was fun to take a job from its beginning, usually a mass of bare earth and construction debris and transform it in just a few days to a good looking finished landscape. It was a perfect job for me, except for the pay and the fact that my wife was so far away. *I needed her uncomfortably, yet so pleasantly close,* "You know the drill".

Here again I was to rub shoulders with some really interesting characters. Bob, my lead man, had the driest and funniest sense of humor of any man I ever knew. Telling us about a tall thin woman that he had met, he described her as follows, "*she wouldn't have had any figure at all, if it weren't for her Adam's apple*", he said. Another time when he was getting old and living behind our house in a small trailer I went out to visit with him. *"Whatcha doin Bob"*, I asked, *"oh I'm just sittin here listening to my arteries get hard"*, he quipped. He had a saying for every occasion, a joke for every situation. Another man, I'll call him "Tommy", was the brunt of many of his jokes. Tommy was an American-born Irishman. He was a clown really, but unlike the clowns in the circus, this clown always had a big grin on his face. Tommy was overweight by at least seventy-five pounds. He had short legs; he didn't look too much unlike a turnip wearing a hat really. He was just a big old teddy bear.

It was almost thirty years ago that I witnessed one of the most hilarious things. It had been raining with just a few snowflakes mixed in to make life miserable. The gravel parking lot was flooded with about eight inches of water and so it was my job to use a backhoe to dig a hole about six feet deep in the middle of the lot down to a loose gravel layer so the water could drain away. Tommy watched me dig the hole and I had shut the engine down on the hoe so that we could shoot the breeze. Tommy was clowning around as usual. It was raining and it was cold. Bob was standing there too as we waited and waited for the water to slowly drain away. Tommy had rubber boots on and a raincoat but it wasn't going to do him any good for what was about to happen.

The parking lot was like a lake about six inches deep. The big hole I had just dug was invisible in the muddy water. There was just me sitting on the backhoe, Bob standing nearby the pile of gravel that I had pulled out of the hole. Tommy was standing next to the backhoe facing me. Can you see it coming? I can still visualize it even after thirty years. Tommy had just made some kind of joke and to emphasize his point; he was waving his arms as he took about three quick steps backwards. Into that hole Tommy went. *"Ooh!"* he gasped, as the cold icy water went over the top of his boots. *"Ooh! Ooh!"* again as it rose to his crotch, then *"Ooh! Ooh! Ooh!"* again as it rose up over his big belly. Instantly, he was up to his ears in that cold icy water and he was thrashing around like a robin in a birdbath. Bob reached him first to help pull him out. "What the hell are you doing in that hole?" he said in his dry, humorous way as he reached out and grabbed Tommy's hand and pulled him up. It didn't take much to pull Tommy up. That water was so cold that he was trying to walk on top of it.

There wasn't much useful work done the rest of that afternoon. Someone gave Tommy a ride home for a hot shower and some dry clothes and the rest of us spent most of our time doubled over laughing. You would have to have to been there to really appreciate the scene of what happened to poor Tommy.

There were other crazy things that Tommy would do. Those of us that were responsible for the jobs were often afraid that he might get us fired. Some of our customers were quite wealthy and those who weren't pretended they were. Most at least pretended that they were sophisticated and here we brought this clown into their midst.

We were landscaping Mrs. Joplin's house at the time. This particular time, Mrs. Joplin was sunbathing in her bikini on her back deck. She had money, she had prestige, she had sophistication and she had a great figure, which wasn't covered very much with that bikini either. Those of us who had passed by her definitely had to concentrate on our tools and our planting plans. Most of those clients thought we, the servants, should be seen but never heard.

There goes Tommy around the corner of the house with me following. Right up on the deck he went with his wheelbarrow and set it down with a thump not over six feet from Mrs. Joplin. "*Mrs. Joplin,*" he said as he stamped his foot, "*what would your mother think if she saw you dressed like that?*" Of course he had a grin on his face and a twinkle in his eye and she hadn't had anyone talk to her like that since she was a teenager, now a long time ago. I was prepared for the worst. I just knew that we were in "*deep doo doo*" now. If there had been a hole nearby I would have crawled into it. Much to my surprise and relief though, she loved it. She loved the attention. It probably made her feel like a teenager again.

A different time, it was just a few blocks away while we were landscaping a big house that Tommy disappeared. The lady of the house was having some kind of lady's tea social. Tommy had disappeared somewhere and I couldn't seem to find him even after a couple of trips around the house. Thinking that perhaps he may have asked the lady if he could use her phone (something we always tried to discourage), I rang the doorbell to see if he was inside the house. "Oh, yes." she said, "He's in the living room talking to the ladies." This was going to be my worst nightmare, I thought, but much to my surprise, everyone seemed to be happy. "Come on in", the lady said. "I'll tell him you're looking for him." There stood Tommy. He was standing there telling the ladies about his experience changing a baby's diaper. He was telling them how he had gotten the mess all over him and gesturing how he had to shake it off his hands and fingers. For all the world he looked like a comedian with a captive audience. I was grateful and relieved to see that all the women were having fun, laughing sometimes to a point where it looked like their sides would split. I didn't think it was funny. I was ready to fire him.

It was almost quitting time before I had a chance to talk to the lady of the house alone. I was very embarrassed as I started to apologize to her about the episode. *"Oh,"she said, "we've never had so much fun. I was thinking about having him over for my next party!"* I was much relieved, that's for sure.

Tommy had his faults, but one of the benefits of having him around was that he always kept us well entertained. Not a day would pass that he couldn't somehow bring us a good laugh or two. Even when we would rake him over the coals for some stupid thing he did, we would be laughing inside privately. He would stick out his lower lip and pout like a little kid. His pouting never lasted very long though. His attention span was only twenty minutes long and soon he would be doing his little elf dance or some other crazy thing to keep us well entertained.

It was in Montana that we all had another good laugh at Tommy's expense. We were doing a short job there planting several thousand willow cuttings along a stream that ran along a new highway project.

The task was a simple one. Just a matter of gathering cuttings from the willows, placing them in bundles so the inspector could count them, and then trudging along the river poking them into whatever open sandy areas we could find.

It was rough country, rocky mountain country. Sometimes the footing was difficult and even a little treacherous. The St. Regis River ran nearby. It was wild and raging with the icy cold water of early spring. It wasn't a big river, hardly ever more than forty feet wide and about three to four feet deep. It was a creek really, but it was wild and young, hell bent for its destiny to join up with the quieter waters of the Clark Fork a few miles downstream. There was still snow to contend with. Most of it was already gone but, in the areas of deep shade or where it had drifted deep during the winter, there were still patches six feet deep or more.

The snow, the raging river; and the sometimes very steep, rocky riverbanks sometimes made it very difficult to get from one place to another to do our work. It was just such difficulties that led to just one more incident with Tommy.

We had worked our way along the steep bluff along the river trying to get from one work-site to another. It was tough going but eventually the slope flattened out a little and now we had a large snowdrift to cross. This was snow that was thawing. It was rotten snow and very few places would hold you up if you tried to walk on it. As luck would have it though, we found a small tree that had fallen across the drift. It was only about twelve inches in diameter but it looked like it would make a pretty good bridge.

We started across with Bob in the lead, then Tommy, then myself and Jon, my middle step-son who worked for us at the time bringing up the rear. It was tedious going. There were branches all along the tree to weave around making it difficult to keep one's balance. Tommy was clowning around as usual and just as you might expect, Tommy slipped right off that log. His arms were flailing around like the rotors on a helicopter, even so he didn't stay airborne for long. Down he went clear up to his fat neck. Turns out that snow was only about two feet thick on top of some brush and it was all melted out underneath. By the time Tommy hit the snow, we were all laughing and when he couldn't get out of his predicament, we just laughed harder. We thought our sides would split.

Try as he might, Tommy couldn't get out of that hole. His feet by now were actually on the ground but he had no way to step up. The brush entangled around his legs was no help. The branches just bent over under his weight each time he tried to step on them. We were in no hurry to pull him out. It was just too much fun as it was. We didn't have the strength anyway because we were laughing so hard. When Tommy would paw at the snow to try to pull himself up, it would just cave in and make the hole a little bigger.

By now he looked for all the world like a big *fat- cheeked prairie dog* with its tail caught in a trap. He knew he wanted to get out of that hole quick, but try as he might, he just couldn't do it. Finally, he gave up and just stood there and started to pout just like a little kid. Out came the lower lip as always. He was getting angry now because we wouldn't help him. "*What am I gonna do, Bob?*" he whined, " *What can I do?*" Bob replied in his usual dry- mannered way, " *Well, Tommy. The first thing I would do would be to get up out of that snow.*" he said. That just brought another round of sidesplitting laughter.

It was one of the funnier things that I have ever seen. It didn't take long to get him out. All he needed was a helping hand. Even without our help, he would have gotten out eventually just by pulling the snow into the hole and working his way to higher ground.

Chapter 16

You've Got To Be Smarter Than The Fish

Bob loved to fish. He was an older man, old enough to be my father in fact. He was a single man and most of his spare time was spent fly-fishing in mountain streams. He seemed to find solace there from the confusion and hustle and bustle of the city where he lived.

Bob never owned any property, just rented a small house or apartment all his life. He never had any children and in a small way at least, I think he thought of me perhaps as the son he never had. He was an honest man as far as I could tell, except for one thing, *he was an alcoholic.* That's something he would never admit, even to himself. He would go six months, a year or even longer and then get drunk and stay drunk for a week or even a month. If the subject of alcohol came up in conversation, he would look you straight in the eye and say "*I haven't had a drink for twenty years*". I think by saying it, he thought that his deep dark secret would go away. He always drank alone and when the bottles were nearly empty, he would call a taxi driver to bring more booze.

Bob and I had worked together for more than a year. I believed he was as dry as a church social. He was my lead man and took on any responsibility I would give him. He was always dependable and he was smart. He had been first in line for my job as foreman but he had passed on it telling the management to give it to me instead. He said he just didn't want the headaches and the responsibilities.

One day, Bob left a message for me at the office that he was coming down with the flu and would be off work for a couple of days. Two, three and then four days passed without any word. The phone calls I made to his number went unanswered. I didn't know much about his private life but I knew he was single and alone. I was beginning to worry about his well-being.

It was with some foreboding that I drove up to his small house. Was he so sick that he couldn't answer the phone? My anxiety increased when I saw the front door was unlocked and slightly open. I knocked on the door and waited for an answer. Knocked again, still no answer. Now, I was really getting worried. I thought the worst; maybe he had met with some foul play. I ran out of options. I knew I was going to have to go in the house, like it or not. Finally, I gathered the courage to walk in. *"Bob? Anybody home?"* I called out. No answer. Called out again, no answer. By now, I was sure we had a problem. I checked out the kitchen, then the living room. I could see the house was pretty messy. I really didn't want to go into the bedroom, afraid of what I might find there. *"Here goes."* I thought, fearing the worst.

I took only a couple of steps into the room and found him lying on his bed. He was half-dressed and the picture didn't look too good, Even when he was healthy, he didn't look very good but now he looked like death personified. He was a heavy smoker, a tall skinny man with skin all wrinkled like a dried prune. I thought he was dead at first. There was no response when I called his name all through the house. I thought someone had done him in. I went to his bedside and touched his arm. It was with much relief that I found his arm was still warm and knew he was still alive.

I tried to figure out what could have happened. I looked quickly around the room and found the answer was right in front of me, plain as the nose on an elephant, a table filled with evidence. A whole group of empty booze bottles and only one with a numbing swallow or two left.

Bob was a good man. He was intelligent and had a sense of humor like no man I ever knew. It was his dark side that I had just now discovered. This is how he fought his demons, rendered senseless by alcohol, drunk and all alone.

Bob and I developed a lasting friendship. It lasted until the day he died in fact, just a few days before his eighty-fourth birthday. We never ever spoke about his problem and if the subject of alcohol came up, he would tell me about his last twenty years of sobriety. The strangest part of the story is, I think he actually believed it.

Most of his other *"fish stories"* you could believe because Bob was a fisherman, and a good one too. It was on a Monday after work that I found out just how good a fisherman he really was. It was on the preceding Friday afternoon that we had a conversation about fishing. *"Would you like some rainbow trout?"* he asked. *"Sure"*, I said "how many do you have?" *"Oh, I haven't caught them yet,"* he replied. *"How many would you like for dinner?"* he added. I could see how this conversation was going. I figured he was pulling my leg. *"Oh, we could eat about twenty-five,"* I said. I figured that would put him in his place.

It was the following Monday afternoon that the topic of fishing came up again. It was just an hour or so before quitting time. "Why don't you stop by the house on the way home," he said, "I've got some fish for you."

I knew from that conversation that I was going to have fish for dinner, but I was hardly prepared for what I saw. There was a sink full of fish, twenty-five of the prettiest rainbow trout that I had seen in one place. I was totally amazed. I had known quite a few fishermen but most of them were a whole lot better at fishing than catching. Most of those fishermen, including myself, could mostly only catch a cold in the nose while fishing even in the best of mountain streams. "How in the world did you catch so many fish?" I wanted to know. "*You've just got to be smarter than the fish!*" he replied, "*and sometimes it helps a little to think like one.*" he added.

There were a lot of stories about Bob's fishing ability. They're too numerous to mention all of them, but I will relate the most notable ones that I witnessed.

We were landscaping a house on Chambers Creek near Tacoma. The creek was actually an outlet for Lake Steilacoom. There was a small dam at the outlet of the lake that controlled the outflow and for that reason, the flow in the creek was almost always the same. Winter, summer, spring or fall, it didn't change the flow very much and for that reason, a deck could be built right at the stream's edge only a few inches above the water. It was fast water, but it only ran a little over a foot deep in most places and only fifteen to twenty feet wide.

It was in the fall. A lot of salmon were spawning in the stream. As babies, they were released from a fish hatchery about four years earlier, just upstream from our work-site. They had now returned for some romance and to meet their destiny.

It was a warm, beautiful fall day when Bob came around the

corner of the house where we were working. *"Have you ever seen anyone catch a fish by hand?"* he asked. *"No"*, I answered, *"and I probably never will."* I was pretty sure he was joking, just *"pulling my leg"* a little bit. *"Follow me and I'll show you how,"* he said, as I followed him around the house to the deck which hung out over the stream. The stream was full of spawning salmon. You could see some fanning out their nests and others resting along the edges of the stream. *"The trick,"* Bob said, *"is to sneak up behind them,* they can only see forward and upward," he added.

I knew from past experiences with Bob that, with his sense of humor, I should expect almost anything. The feeling I got was that he was probably setting me up for a joke, and that if I wasn't careful, I could end up looking like a fool. With some amusement, I watched him get down on all fours and slowly started creeping out onto the deck. As he got near the edge of the deck, he started to drag himself slowly along the edge in an upstream direction. He finally paused awhile and ever so slowly, hung his head and right shoulder over the edge. It was just as if it all took place in slow motion. I couldn't see his arm and hand from where I was standing but I knew that things were getting serious. Bob was stretched out very still now and a long time passed before his next move. To my absolute amazement, he raised his arm and in his hand was a salmon. He had a good grip on it, just in front of its tail, as he stood to his feet. It was not as big a salmon as they sometimes get, perhaps just eight or ten pounds, but still it was impressive. The salmon wasn't very happy about the whole thing but the rest of us were very impressed, I can tell you that for sure. Bob held the fish high for everyone to see and then put it back in the water where it swam away unharmed.

We were spellbound. "How did you do that?" we asked. "Nothing to it," he said, "the trick is to just slide your fingers up alongside of their tail and tickle their sides with your fingers. The fish just thinks a willow twig is brushing past and when the opportunity seems right, all you have to do is clasp your hand around the fish and pull it out of the water." Easy for him to say, but I'm still amazed.

It was a different time and a different place that I was to witness Bob's fishing expertise again. We were on a job in South Dakota, out on the prairies. It's barren out there for those of us used to the mountains and trees in the West. We were getting homesick.

It was a day off, a Sunday that we decided to find some trees. The nearest trees in any quantity were over one hundred-fifty miles away in the Black Hills. It was a long way but we decided it would be worth the drive. It was in the Rapid City area that we found the trees. They were pine trees mostly and we thought the place was a piece of heaven.

We found a small stream that ran through the countryside. Since Bob carried his fishing pole everywhere he went, he decided that he would like to go fishing. We found a small sporting goods store along the way where Bob bought a four day fishing license and supplies.

Bob was a fly fisherman. He had utter disdain for bait fishing. "I want to buy some flies," he said to the proprietor. The store owner was just trying to be helpful when he said, "You won't catch any fish with flies here this time of year," he said. "If I have to use bait, I won't go fishing," Bob grumbled back. Looking through the selection of flies, it took him a little while to find what he wanted to buy. He paid the man and said, "Let's go fishing!" as we walked out the door.

This was the first time I had ever actually watched Bob fish. It was obvious right away that he was an expert. In only a little over an hour of fishing, he had caught his limit. It was probably the first time anyone ever caught their limit in that stream in a long, long time I would wager. It wasn't because his equipment was fancy. Most of it was just ordinary except for his fishing pole. It was an expensive one. He was quite proud of that. He fished with a short line. No fancy casting for him. "There's just as many fish on my side of the river as there are on the other", he would say. The flies he used were just the old-fashioned ones and sometimes, they were all worn out with hardly any feathers left on them. He claimed that all that new fancy stuff being sold to fishermen were designed just to catch the fishermen. "*If you want to catch your limit, you just have to be smarter than the fish*", he always insisted.

The only other time that I was able to watch Bob fish was on the trip home from South Dakota. We had taken a small three-day job planting trees for the Montana Highway Department. The job was right along the Montana-Idaho border planting the trees at a highway interchange. It was the same river that I wrote about earlier. It was the St. Regis River but unlike when we had been there before, it was now tame and just right for fishing.

It was a convenient job. It was on the route home from our South Dakota job so we were making the most of it. We were staying about forty miles east of the job that Saturday night and the plan was to drive out to the work-site Sunday morning to look over the site and plan Monday's work. We knew that we would have a lot of time to kill, the whole day in fact. Figuring that it would be a good time for Bob to do a little fishing.

We stopped at a store on the way to the job-site so Bob could buy his three-day fishing license and proceeded on to look over the job-site. We only spent about two hours at the site but we were satisfied that we had seen enough and headed for the river.

It was fun to watch Bob fish. It took him a little while to rig up.

Some of the flies he was tying on looked like they were twenty years old, but you could tell real quick that he was an expert in everything he did as regards to fishing.

Bob only made one or two casts in any one spot, always in the fast water. If he didn't get a fish to raise for the fly, he would just move on to the next spot. Almost immediately, he started to catch fish as he moved along, scrambling over the big boulders that lined the riverbank.

Every so often, we would pass by some other fishermen who would ask, "Are you having any luck?" "No, they're just not biting today", Bob would answer back, even though he almost had his limit by then. It was an inside joke for Bob. He loved to hear those other fishermen say, "There just doesn't seem to be any fish in the river", or "It must be too hot today", or too cloudy or some other thing.

This was the sort of thing Bob thought was funny. Bob's sense of humor was different. He liked to play along and listen to the stories, the excuses for not catching fish when all the while, his creel was nearly full.

It wasn't long before it was time to leave the river. Bob had caught his limit and it was time to go. I really enjoyed that day. I knew I had watched a man who was most likely the best in the world at the sport of fishing. I had been watching a champion. I knew without any doubt whatsoever that here was a man who was indeed "smarter than the fish".

I think Bob was as intelligent as any man I ever knew but along with his problem with alcohol, he also had another addiction. It was tobacco that had him hooked, he was a very heavy smoker. He lived a long life though, even so, almost until his eighty-fourth birthday but I can tell you for sure that he didn't die an easy death.

To say that the last four years of his life was less than miserable would be a terrible lie. Suffocating to death over a four year period is a hard way to go.

It all starts with a shortness of breath, then soon to follow, great difficulty just to walk across the room.

Oxygen delivery to the house and its use by the patient buys a little time but soon that doesn't bring very much relief from the gradual but nevertheless deadly suffocation. It was my misfortune to watch him waste away to a mere skeleton and die. In Bob's case, even with the use of oxygen, it was only a short time until he became "bedridden". He would just lie there panting with a look of panic in his eyes, fighting for every breath. Did you know that oxygen is required to digest food? Many times he would just lie there gasping after even the slightest bit of food was digesting. It took four years but I repeat again, "it's a very hard way to die". A heavy smoker I was myself, about thirty five years ago, I quit, "Thank God" for that. After watching Bob die the way he did over a four year period I can say with the utmost conviction that if you *"don't smoke, don't start"*. *If you do smoke, do yourself and those that care about you a favor and "quit"*. When I was a smoker, I too had the cavalier attitude that everyone must die, "so what's the big deal", now I know that *"how we die"* demands much more respect.

Chapter 17

Getting Settled

I got way out ahead of myself in this story, telling about Tommy and Bob. My wife isn't going to be very happy with me if I don't pick up the story where I left her in California.

In about March, I moved to Washington with my new job. Joy couldn't leave California until she had completed her commitment to her teaching contract in late June. It was a long four months and I missed her terribly. We got together a few times, whenever a long holiday weekend came about I would either go see her or she would come to see me. I was single a long time before I married her and I really liked and appreciated having a *life-mate*. And *yes, you're right, it was and still is a thrill to get uncomfortably yet pleasantly close enough to smell that perfume, just one small dab behind each ear.*

I was getting settled into my new job by the end of June. It certainly wasn't a good paying job, but I really liked the work. It seemed like every day was an adventure even though it was a *rinky-dink outfit* that I worked for. The inefficiency of the whole outfit led me to mistakenly believe that the landscaping business was a veritable gold mine. I thought if these people could make it in business, anybody could. Of course, I didn't know that all the while they were slowly going broke.

Joy packed some of our worldly goods, and headed for our new home. She brought with her just some essentials all loaded in a U-haul trailer behind her car as well as the three boys and our two dogs, *Lassie and Blackie*. We settled into a little house, a shack really, only about twelve miles from where we live today. Poor Joy, she grew up with a live-in maid in a beautiful home and now, here she was, living in a shack with three boys and me. We were just happy to be together again and eager to get on with our lives. Moving was a lot simpler in my old bachelor days. After going through the big flood on the Eel River in 1964 followed by the hotel fire at Orleans California, I didn't have very much left to move. Even though by then I was thirty two-years old, at the time, my personal possessions could quite easily fit into a couple of average sized cardboard boxes. Not so today, the house is full, the garage, shop and basement are all full. All of it "*yesterday's treasures*" but a lot of it just "*today's junk*".

The three boys aged thirteen, fifteen and sixteen, weren't happy at all. We didn't blame them. It's a tough age to be uprooted from your comfort zone. The change of schools, friends left behind, unfamiliar surroundings, were all pretty traumatic for them. It's hard too, for kids to have a step-parent who seems to always get in their way. Joy and I were glad to get them away from California. Drugs were just getting into the schools there and we felt that we were leaving in the nick of time. It all became moot when we later learned that drugs had started to appear in Washington schools as well. The boys adapted though. Eventually, they grew up, like all kids and left one-by-one to go out into the big wide world to seek their destiny.

It was August before we found a house to buy, the same house we live in to this day. It was a small house by today's standards but one we could afford. A short time after we bought the house, I went to California to get the rest of our household goods. It was a long trip back in a U-haul truck. It made me wish I had some stock in an oil company. It seemed that I had to stop at every service station on the highway for a fill-up. That old truck was a *thirsty old "gasaholic"*.

Moving is a trying task. It was a real relief to get moved in and settled down. I told Joy that once was enough. I didn't intend to ever move again. We've lived here thirty-three years now and have no intentions to move.

Chapter 18

On the Job Training

I didn't actually need any training to do the work of landscaping. My earlier years as a kid on the farm and later as a logger and equipment operator, had trained me quite well. It was just a matter of looking at the job, deciding what was needed and then get it done. I could see very early on that, in the *world of contracting*, we only got paid for one thing and that was *work completed*.

Mostly, I just trained myself to deal with people. They were always the biggest problem. I had a lot to learn in that area. I was to rub shoulders with a lot of interesting characters through the landscaping business. Some of them were in management, some of them were on my crew and some of them were the customers. I think most groups of people fall under the *80/20 rule*. Twenty percent of any group will give you eighty percent of your grief. It also holds true that twenty percent of the people you know will probably give you about eighty percent of all the rewards that you'll ever get in life.

In our crew were Bob, Tommy, and George. George was a grizzled up old guy. Sometimes I thought that maybe we were giving him welfare because he never did seem to do very much work. He couldn't spell either. One day he got mad at one of his co-workers about something. He was really telling him off. He was sputtering and shaking his old, crooked fingers in the guy's face, "————and if you don't like it," he said, "that's just tee-uff-uff tough." Then, just to make his point, he repeated it again. "That's just tee-uff-uff tough."

There were other characters on our crew too. One of the guys had to be bailed out of jail a time or two and another would go on a big drunk every month or so.

And there was the upper management. You would think that in their position they might have a few brains, but that wasn't always the case. We were moving a large tree one day. It was about forty-feet tall with a trunk about sixteen inches in diameter. We estimated that this tree weighed about thirty-five tons including a ten-foot root ball. We were planning to use a sixty-ton crane to swing it into place when word came down from one of the bosses that we should try to slide it over on sheets of plywood. He had seen this done with a four hundred-pound plant some place and he was quite sure it would work. He left out the most important part, how were we going to lift it on to the plywood and how were we going to push it over to its new position? I couldn't believe my ears. I was thinking perhaps, if his brains were exploding dynamite, he wouldn't even have enough to pass wind.

He was one of the owners. It seemed that he was always interfering with the work. He was interfering with one of my jobs one day when I locked horns with him. He thought I was kind of uncouth when I told him to stay in the office and push his pencils. I didn't endear myself much to him, but at least he stayed off my jobs after that.

Thirty five ton tree on the move

Then, there were the customers. They also came in all types. Sometimes, she might be a little old lady on social security. We were almost ashamed to do the work for fear that she couldn't afford it. Often, that type of person would be waving a check under your nose before you even finished the job or gave her a bill. Sometimes, it was the guy with two luxury cars in the garage plus a sports car. Try to get money out of him and he might tell you, *"Well, I'll have to transfer some money out of one of my accounts, but I'm leaving for Europe in the morning and,"* ————, *and,* ————, *and,* ————.

One customer was a doctor who was trying to build a 25,000 square foot mansion despite the fact he was going to go bankrupt.

He was a highly respected doctor, said to be brilliant, in fact, but he must have checked his brains at the clinic's door because he didn't seem to have any common sense anywhere else. He never did complete the house. In fact, he went bankrupt leaving a lot of contractors unpaid and the house to be repossessed by the bankers. When it was all over, he overdosed on drugs in an attempt to commit suicide. He even botched that up and survived.

There was the financier, who built a 17,000 square foot house. This guy could afford it. The $4 million price tag was just peanuts for him. He and his wife were wonderful people to work for. Everyone got paid correctly and on time and the job always ran smoothly. They even threw a party for all the workers when the job was completed.

And, there was the lady who was complaining about all those nasty loggers raping the forests. All the while, we were building a monster deck for her. The deck was first class of many terraces stepping down the hillside, it cost about $35,000 and was constructed out of the very best, fine-grained old growth cedar. Apparently no one ever told her that lumber comes from trees.

My on-the-job training taught me a lot of important things, but two really are etched into my mind. Number one: *Never work for a lawyer or psychologist*, unless you can afford it. If you do, you'll end up doing more work and get paid less than your contract. Number two: *Never work for a lawyer or psychologist*. Oh, maybe that's a little harsh. I suppose the 80/20 rule applies to them also.

Chapter 19

New Challenges

It was a busy life for me. We now had two cute little girls to raise. The outfit I originally started working for was in a financial pinch and sold out to a bigger outfit. Now the jobs were spread out over a much larger area making for much longer commutes. It wasn't unusual at all for the alarm to go off at 4:00 AM and most of the time, I didn't return home until about six or seven PM. Joy was a true gem. No matter how early we got up, she would always rise with me and make my breakfast. We always cherished that time together, just an hour or so each morning, before I went off to work.

The larger outfit decided to give it up too. The red ink was even more than they could handle. It took awhile to complete all the jobs that were lined up and previously contracted. During that time, one of our superintendents started up another outfit backed by Toro, the lawnmower people, as soon as our jobs were completed I followed him to the new outfit.

It was a different kind of work. It was erosion control and most

Erosion control equipment / hydroseeder and hydromulch on semi-trailer

of the jobs were on construction projects, most notably, highway construction. There were only three of us involved at first. The "head honcho", a man to do the office work, and me, as the field superintendent.

The business grew and grew and soon I was "*in the soup*" again. The very thing I moved to Washington for, to be home every night as a family man was for naught. Soon we had jobs in Eastern Washington followed by jobs in Oregon, Idaho, Montana, Wyoming, Colorado, Alaska and South Dakota.

We did the best we could under the circumstances. I remember one time when Joy came to visit me for the weekend in Pendleton, Oregon. It was somewhat of an ordeal for her. We had two baby girls, one about six months and the other eighteen months old. She had to change trains at Portland, no easy task when you consider two babies, strollers, bottles, diapers etc. When she got off the train at Pendleton she was all worn out, after 5 hours dealing with those two babies and all their stuff plus her own baggage. Those weren't the easiest of times, but we got by and looking back today it seems that it was sort of an adventure.

That little company was getting bigger and bigger and company politics was rearing its ugly head. The office and support personnel were beginning to outnumber the people in the field doing the work. I had more experience now and I could see the red ink coming. No one wanted to hear what I had to say. They were really more interested in gaining position and power than profit for the company. It was only about a year that I worked for that company. I was on the wrong side of the politics and it was time to go.

The business manager was off on a trip the day that I left. We had been friends a long time and I still felt some loyalty to him so I composed a long letter that I left on his desk. The letter contained an outline of the problems as I saw them, some warnings and some predictions. I knew that it would fall on deaf ears but I was making one last try. Then, out the door I went, never to return.

Chapter 20

A New Beginning

Only a few days had passed when I got a call from Bob, my old friend the fisherman. "I just heard through the grapevine that you've quit your job and you're out of work, is that true?" he asked. "Yes, it is." I answered. "Good," he said, "why don't you come to work with me?"

Bob had been doing some freelance landscape work and wanted a partner to form a little company. It sounded like a pretty good idea to me. I was out of work anyway so I didn't have a whole lot to lose. The companies that I had been working for never provided me with very much security or wealth. Maybe it was time to try business on my own. Bob and I had always gotten along well too. It seemed that we could enjoy working together as partners.

The landscaping business is an easy business to get into. All you need is a business license, contractor's license, a few tools, a wheelbarrow, a strong back and a weak mind. A pick-up truck is also a must-have and it helps if a person can read an architect's plans.

Soon, we had our own little company. The jobs were small, the profits even smaller but at least we had some control over our destiny. It was just a short time until the jobs started to get larger; the cash flow increased and of course, so did the bills. Eventually, we added another partner and incorporated the business.

About nine months passed when I received a call from the business manager of the erosion control outfit where I resigned. We chatted awhile, as friends always do but I knew that he had something more important on his mind. *"What have you been doing lately?"* I asked. *"Well, I've been reading about the rise and fall of the Roman Empire,"* he said. *"And that's pretty much what happened to us."* he added, "the Toro Company has decided to close our doors, seems that there was more red ink than they could handle."

I wasn't too surprised. I had been hearing some rumors that they were in trouble. I felt kind of bad about the whole thing actually, but in spite of that there was some small satisfaction in knowing that my beliefs had been vindicated, and my predictions had come true. It was proof once again to me that in the world of contracting, *money came from only one thing and that is work completed.*

The conversation eventually got around to the reason for his call. Toro wanted to close the books but needed someone to complete the jobs that were still outstanding. These were just a few small jobs, three in Montana, two each in Idaho and Washington State and one in South Dakota.

These were good jobs for us. We were select bidders and as such, we got good prices for the work. The same jobs that were losers for Toro were a bonanza for us. They simply had too much overhead. They had a big office loaded with personnel. They had company cars for almost anyone who could spell their name. They had car phones at a time when they were still rare. They had expense accounts with martini lunches and the occasional trip to seminars to cities like San Francisco that just happened to coincide with the schedule of the most renowned football games. We were quite a contrast in our little enterprise. Our contribution was just a couple of rusty pickup trucks, a few picks, rakes and shovels and the ever-present wheelbarrow. We didn't have expense accounts for a martini lunch but rather a brown bag and a few chug-a-lugs out of the almost always present garden hose.

Chapter 21

North to Alaska

Time passed quickly as is the *nasty* habit of time. We never made a whole lot of money but still we managed to make a living. Independence and the satisfaction of being self-employed were our biggest rewards, worth a whole lot more to me than the little bit of security gained while working for others, even though it may never buy a man a luxury car or a swimming pool.

It wasn't long before things really started to *go to hell* in the proverbial *hand-basket*. Work became as scarce as *truth in a political campaign*, as *rare as a penguin in Tucson, Arizona*. With the ever-decreasing amount of work available it became very difficult to bid a job high enough to make any money. We were not alone in our misery. Contractors all around us were in trouble, many of them gave up and went bankrupt.

I was in despair when John called, (he was the man that was my boss while I worked for the erosion control outfit, their business manager). We had laid off our workers and once again, I had no meaningful work. All the available jobs were just bid in too cheap.

"I'm putting a job together on the Alaska Pipeline." John said, "I was wondering if you might be interested." Sure I was interested, to say the least. Anything that might stave off bankruptcy and starvation even for a little while seemed like a good deal to me. "I'm dealing with a company in Alaska who needs people who have done erosion control work," he went on. "They want someone to help them bid a job on the pipeline and if they get the job, they'll need somebody to help with the management," he added.

This was the break that I needed. Bob had already retired prior to our hard times but I had a family to support and bills to pay. I needed work and soon. My emotions were mixed as we approached the airport at Fairbanks. One side of me was saying that this was an opportunity to make a living for my family. The other side was saying, why should I take a job over 2,000 miles from home which would entail long separations from them. In the end, I had no real choice except to accept the challenge. I needed the job; my family needed the money.

It was a long day bidding that job. The job itself was a big one, about 150 miles of pipeline erosion control and revegetation. There were the haul roads, the waste areas, storage yards, the borrow pits and the pipeline right-of- way itself, all had to be restored with vegetation.

At the end of the day an agreement was struck, John would get a finder's fee and the other two of us would be hired to help run the job. This would all be moot however if the company failed the bid and the job would then go to a competing company.

A couple of weeks went by before we received the call. It was good news. The bid was accepted by Alyeska (the consortium who built the pipeline) and it was time to go to work.

Once again it was time to leave the family behind, just what I had originally planned not to do. It was a whole different world I met when I stepped out of the plane at Fairbanks with a whole new cast of characters to meet. The company that I was about to sign on with was a family enterprise owned by three brothers and their mother. They were from the South originally, Florida, in fact. Though they had been in Alaska awhile, some of their Southern ways were still very apparent. These were tough-minded and self-determined men but I was always amused to hear how they deferred to their mother.

I never got to know her very well, but I could tell that she played a strong role in management decisions though she was never highly visible. It was fun to hear the eldest brother, who was the business manager, discuss some urgent problem with her on the phone. *"Yes, Mama,"* he would say. *"Yes, Mama! No! Mama. Yes, Mama. No Mama. But dammit Mama! Yes Mama!"*

One thing I noticed early on was that most of these conversations ended with "Yes, Mama." You could tell right off that she held a very strong position with the company decisions from behind the scenes.

Chapter 22

Camp Life

It was about ninety miles out to the "Big Delta" construction camp. The first colorful character I ran into was a driver sent to give me a ride out to camp. She was a teamster (truck driver). She was an old hand about the camp and she didn't waste any time being a lady. She probably outweighed me by twenty pounds, not much fat, mostly muscle. "*Where's your bags?*" she asked. "*I'll go get them,*" I said. "*No!*" she said, "*That's my job*". *Just shut up and get in the cab of the pickup.*" This embarrassed me a little but the last thing I wanted to do was stand there and argue with her in front of everybody else. "*Prudence is the best part of valor,*" I thought as I climbed in the pickup. On the way out to camp, she filled me in on all the camp details. She was actually quite friendly. Mostly she just wanted to let me know that she was a "*pipe-liner*" and as tough and *macho* as any man. She was a big blond, about twenty-six years old. She had a good collection of four letter words, which she sprinkled generously into every sentence she uttered. She could tell that I wasn't used to hearing this from the mouth of a woman. She knew it embarrassed

Delta Camp / ninety miles south of Fairbanks

me a little so she poured it on. By the time we got to Big Delta Camp, I had heard it all and wouldn't have been surprised by anything.

Delta was a big camp; twelve hundred people were in residence there. Someone told me it was the ninth largest city in the state of Alaska and it had its share of characters. There were quite a few women sprinkled around among the work crews. Some of them were inspectors for the government or Alyeska, some were teamsters and quite a few worked in the kitchen. A few of the women could spit out profanities that would shame almost any drunken sailor and some of them remained very much ladylike in their demeanor.

There was the tall blonde *grease monkey*. Her job was to change oil and lubricate the heavy equipment. We would see her on the job in coveralls, greasy coveralls from head to foot and then we would see her in camp all cleaned up. A beautiful young woman about twenty-four years old and *very much a lady*.

There was the little Jewish girl about twenty-three years old, small in stature but tall in character and very much a lady. She was a lot of fun, one of those people who could always make you laugh even when things had gone awry. Life was all fun for her but she took her job seriously as an inspector for Alyeska. We were all stunned one evening in the mess hall while having dinner. Down the aisle between the tables she came, thump, thump, thump in backwards somersaults. She then stood up, bowed to the tables to the right and then to the left and without even cracking a smile, walked slowly out of the room. She certainly got our attention with her stunt. We later learned that she had taken some kind of course at a clown school, intending to become a clown. The reason that she pulled her stunt in the mess hall was that one of her friends had dared her to do it. True to her personality, she took her friend up on the dare.

And there was the *"Wicked Woman"*. She managed the warehouse where we had to pick up our supplies. I never knew her real name. I didn't need to as her nickname described her perfectly. She had the most vulgar vocabulary of anyone I ever knew, male or female. *Every sentence she uttered was laced with four letter words.* She definitely had the ability to raise vulgarity to unsurpassable heights.

There were a lot of other colorful women in camp, some whose goal in life was to appear more macho than the men. In some ways, who could blame them? After all they were trying to make their mark in a man's world and it couldn't have been easy.

We had a lot of interesting men in camp too. The men in my crew were no small exception. The men in my crew varied in age from eighteen to sixty. The intelligence level varied on a *few* of them just about as much, somewhere between the high zeros to the low one hundreds. My job would have been much easier had I been trained as a *school playground monitor*. Any woman can tell you that men are just little boys who have grown up, but I had a few in my crew who never did grow up.

There was our field mechanic. He was the oldest man in our crew. He was responsible for the on-site repairs for the machinery and equipment and was an expert at keeping it all operational usually under very difficult conditions. We held him in very high esteem but unfortunately, he had an inferiority complex. The slightest thing would send him into a snit and he would pout and sulk for two or three days. It was normal for him to whine and bellyache for thirty minutes whenever we presented something to him for repair. He would whine about the stupid "*blankety-blank*" no good operator who broke it, or the *grease monkey* who didn't lubricate it correctly, *or those of us who were in charge* failing to look after the equipment properly. One day my frustrated boss asked me "What the hell's the matter with that guy anyway?" "Well, he's overworked," I replied. "What makes you think that?" he went on. "Well," I said, "every time something breaks, he has to fix it twice". "First, he has to fix the blame and usually it takes him as long to do that as it does to make the repair." We had a good laugh over that and it became our inside joke. From then on, whenever the mechanic would get into a snit my boss and I would look at each other and say, "*Oh, he's just overworked because he has to fix everything twice.*"

There were the "*Three Stooges*". They ranged in age from about twenty-five to thirty-five but their maturity was about the same as sixth to eighth graders in a school-yard. They adhered to the premise that if they could gang up on a fellow worker and make him look inferior, somehow, they in turn, would somehow seem to be superior. *Does this not sound like some of the kids you knew in the school-yard at recess?*

It came to pass that the youngest man to join the Operating Engineers Union in Alaska was hired as an equipment operator. His father was one of the head honchos of Alyeska and his employment had some political considerations.. "Take good care of him," my boss said, "keep him out of trouble until he learns the ropes." It turned out that this new kid wasn't any trouble at all. He was a good worker. He was smart and eager to master any equipment that I put in his charge.

He only made one major mistake while he worked for me. He told one of those three stooges who his father was and his father's position held with Alyeska. From that day on, they did everything in their power to make that new kid look bad. One day, the kid was loading a huge machine on a lowboy trailer for transport. This machine was four feet wider than the trailer and only about six inches of those big balloon tires rode the trailer on each side. The remainder of the tires just hung out there in space. It was impossible to see over the hood and the wheels of this machine, anything at all closer than fifty feet. The custom was for someone to stand out front and give the operator signals while loading. It was virtually impossible to load it without sliding off the trailer without the help of a signal-man.

This was the scene as I drove up in the pickup that day. The three stooges were standing around giggling and laughing, refusing to give the kid any guidance of any kind in the loading. The kid was desperately going to give loading the rig a try, even though it would have been a mistake on his part. If he had been an older, more experienced man, he would have simply waited and let those three stooges just make a bigger fool of themselves.

My arrival was none too soon. It was plain to see that a disaster was soon to happen. The kid had already started to load by the time

I climbed up on the trailer gooseneck to give him hand signals for guidance. The kid was very grateful of course and much relieved as we continued the loading process without further incident

There was never any real danger to the operator doing the loading, but the costs of damaged equipment and down time incurred while reloading could be substantial. I had seen this machine slip off the lowboy trailer just a few weeks before. A very experienced man was operating it. Even so, it had gotten away from him, causing damage, lost time and expense.

As soon as I had a chance to speak to my young equipment operator in private, I explained to him that under no circumstances was he to take risks with the equipment or himself just to placate someone's amusement. As for the three stooges, I told them that they were acting like children and should be ashamed of themselves. Scolding them had about the same effect as pouring water on a duck. They just didn't really care.

There were other characters too. There was a writer who spent hours and hours at night writing a novel. True to form, the troublemakers did everything possible to make him look bad. He was a different sort. He was British for one thing, direct from England. He was educated too, which automatically made him a target for the bullies and troublemakers. He belonged to the Laborers Union and completed any task I gave him in a complete and judicious manner.

Reading this part of the story may make you wonder how the pipeline ever got completed. It got finished because there were over twenty thousand men and women on the job and the eighty-twenty rule was in effect as usual.

This was a colossal project, the largest I believe for Americans since the Panama Canal. Sure there were the misfits and malcon-

Landscaping the pipeline / tree planting preparation

tents but there were literally hundreds of dedicated men and women who gave the project their all. It was an engineering achievement, a construction marvel and an operational success.

The value of a column of oil traveling eight miles per hour through a *four-foot* diameter pipe *twenty-four hours per day three-hundred-sixty-five days per year* is astronomical. If the oil stops flowing as is bound to happen someday as the oil reserves dry up, the price of fuel and energy will go up. We owe a lot to the investors, the engineers, the managers and the workers, from the men and women at the top to the ones at the bottom. They all made a contribution to the pipeline for our well being, every day.

There were five different camps that my crew and I resided in during my employment on the pipeline. Since we didn't work for Alyeska but for a sub-contractor instead, we were actually just guests at the camps during our stays. Each camp had its own colorful cast of characters besides our crew and they and their stories provided most of the entertainment.

Watering a sand-cut slope to make the grass grow

No story about the Alaska Pipeline would be complete without a few bear stories, *"encounters of the bear kind"*. The first bear story is about a *"bare"* naked man and a *"black bear"*. We had a lot of bears around the camps that were north of the Yukon River. The ones we saw the most were *"camp bears"*. They were always hungry, tame enough to be a big nuisance and wild enough to be dangerous. These bears would spend a lot of time under and around the barracks and some of them were wily enough to get inside.

At Five Mile Camp, they got to be such a nuisance that all the barracks doors had to be fitted with a door guard around the latch so the bears could not get in.

The *"bear"* and *"bare"* story takes place in one of the barracks. One day, a bear broke into one of the barracks to look for some food while at the same time, one of the men was taking a shower in the shower room. The bear wasn't really looking for any trouble and neither was the guy in the shower but sooner or later the two were going to have a little impromptu meeting.

Black bear on the prowl for food / "a doughnut would be nice"

Bears don't really see very well at all but rather rely on their sense of smell for everything. This poor bear was just sniffing along hoping to find a doughnut left over from someone's breakfast. All at once, this poor unsuspecting "*bare*" guy stepped out of the shower and came face-to-face with a real live "*bear*". The bear was horrified *(must have been a young maiden bear)*. The man was *terrified* and they both took off in opposite directions in a hell of a hurry. It was surely a sight to behold. At least the bear had the decency to wear a fur coat.

The next bear story took place in the same camp. I was in my room doing paperwork. It was normal for me to fill out the daily reports for all the different jobs we were doing as well as employee time cards, etc. I had a small desk in my room and if I happened to be in the vicinity of the barracks in the middle of the day, I would stop in and eat my lunch and catch up on my reports. It was peaceful and quiet in camp during the day as all the "*pipe-liners*" were out on the job.

All at once the peace was shattered by some kind of ruckus down in the recreation room at the other end of the barracks. It

"Yes, this is nice but I'd really rather have a doughnut"

was one of the bullcooks who cleaned the barracks. He was cussing and yelling at the top of his lungs. It took a little while for me to get out of my room and down the hall to where all the commotion was coming from. The party was just about over by the time I came on the scene. That poor black bear was just going out the door and the bullcook was whacking him hard across the rear with a cue stick. Lucky for the bullcook that this room had pool tables with plenty of cue sticks. After everything settled down, I examined that cue stick. I could see that the butt end of it had teeth marks punctured almost halfway through. I knew right then that if I had been that bullcook, I would have just let that bear have that recreation room and the rest of the barracks if he wanted it. I would have been looking for much safer ground.

You can't blame the bullcook for putting up a fight though. *Bears were the bullcook's nemesis.* Bears can make an awful mess when they get inside a building and whatever mess they made, the bullcook would have to clean up. Bears have the ability to destroy almost anything with their claws and if they can't think of anything else to do that is worthwhile, they will *"poop"* all over the place on the way

"It seems like there should be a little doughnut in here someplace"

out the door.

That's all the bear stories that I am going to tell in this book. If you want more bear stories, you'll have to read my other book, *When Fast Food Was a Rabbit.* You'll find more of them there.

By the time I left the pipeline, the job was winding down. Some of the camps had already closed. The work force that had been some twenty thousand personnel at its peak had now dwindled to five or six thousand. It was time for me to go too. My job was complete and I was tired. For seven days a week, twelve hours a day, I had worried about the company owner's investment, their resources, men and equipment long enough, it was time to go home and get some rest. It was time to go home and be a complete family again. It was time to spend some good times with Joy and those two little girls.

Completed "above ground" section of pipeline

Chapter 23

New Beginnings, Again!

After I returned from work on the pipeline, I turned again to landscaping for my living. This time around, I formed a little company under my own name and worked mostly by myself. This work was almost risk free. I could pick and choose the jobs that suited me best and I didn't have to worry about any payroll to meet. It got lonesome of course when I worked alone, especially if I was faced with building a thirty-ton rock wall or when faced with a twelve-ton pile of dirt to move with a wheelbarrow.

My two daughters were growing up and soon they were big enough to do some of the lighter work on Saturdays and holidays to earn some spending money. I also teamed up with other small contractors to do the heavier and larger jobs.

Eventually a grandson, Josh, was added to the family mix. I'll just call him "Dummy" in this story because it's what I called him when we worked together. It was all in fun of course but it did sort of become his nickname.

He was only nine years old when Dummy started to work with

"Oops", "oh well, maybe we can landscape the sky"

me. The main reason I kept him busy was that I knew busy hands and minds seldom get into trouble, *(my mother in her wise way,* used to say *"idle hands are the Devil's workshop")* Besides, I always enjoyed his company. Sometimes, I would arrange my work so that we could work weekends and most holidays to keep him busy and so we could work together.

I gave him light chores at first but as he grew in stature and strength, his skills improved and I kept adding to his challenges. At first it was simply *"Dummy, go to the pickup and bring me a round point shovel,"* often followed by *"Not that one, Dummy. I wanted the other one."* Or it might be, *"Go get the broom, Dummy,"* followed by, *"Don't stand there like a Dummy, get busy and sweep the sidewalk and patio."*

A nice landscape—man made stream

We had one of those rare relationships, Josh and I. It didn't seem to matter a whole lot what I challenged him with, he would rise to meet the challenge and I would pour it on him. He grew stronger, older and more mature and it seemed hardly any time at all until he was driving the front-end loader and ditching machinery for landscape irrigation.

He worked his way through high school as *Dummy*. He worked his way through college to a bachelor's degree and I still called him *Dummy*. It wasn't until he got his master's degree in business that I quit calling him *Dummy*. He calls me *Dummy* now and I think that he has earned the right.

We had many good times together. When he was about twenty years old, we went on a camping trip to Alaska. It was sometime in early August. The work had come to a stand-still for about three weeks. Maybe we could go to Alaska, I thought. It would be fun to show Josh where I had been some years before. He thought it was a good idea. I think he thought it would be good to see if old *"Gramps"* had been telling him the truth or not, perhaps see if some

Josh (Dummy) at college graduation

of his yarns might be a little *stretched.*

It was quite an undertaking. The trip would be over five thousand miles so I knew I should talk it over with Joy before making a final commitment. As usual, in Joy's most generous way, she said, "Sure, I think it will be good for both of you". So the plan began.

It took four or five days of preparation to get ready to go. The first job was to build a platform of plywood 8 x 8 foot square on the back of the pickup truck. We built storage areas underneath for food and supplies and all the other gear needed for a long-extended camping trip. We purchased a cheap 8 x 8 foot "pop-up" tent to put on top of the platform. Joy bought enough food and supplies for the two of us to last a month. She bought anything

"Dummy" and our "home away from home"

non-perishable that she could find, from canned fruit to popcorn, from beef jerky to canned pork and beans to dried fruit. We were all set to live *"high on the hog"*, I can tell you for sure.

It was a one-of-a-kind camping outfit. It was different but it worked very well. A tarp went over the whole thing while in transit so it didn't look too bad. At the end of each day, we would simply uncover the load, pop up the tent, set out a makeshift table for the camp stove and we were ready to camp.

It was a great adventure. This was my third trip up and down the Alcan Highway. It was much improved now, paved all the way, but when I traveled on it during the days of the pipeline, nine hundred miles of it was just gravel. When Joy, Kathy, Susie and I traveled it before towing a 32 foot trailer, it was either mud or dust with little else in between.

I discovered Alaska was a far different place now from back in the pipeline days. Now the highways and byways were filled with tour buses and tourists. The pipeline had become a tourist attrac-

Mama and her baby, somewhere in the Yukon Territory, Canada

tion along with the gold mines etc. It was quite a change from when I had been there before. In those days it was all pipeline and construction equipment.

It was a great trip. By the time we got back home, we had seen some of the best scenery in the world, nearly 5,000 miles of it. We stayed only one night in a motel and ate only two meals in restaurants. All the rest were spent in our tent with our camp-stove. It was an adventure and a trip to always remember.

Al Brice on right and myself in front of our tent all folded down ready for travel. Fairbanks Alaska

Chapter 24

A falling tree, A wet behind

Josh and I took another trip, just the two of us. It lasted only four days but it was unforgettable. It was a camping and kayaking trip to Canada. I was old enough to know better and he was a wide-eyed energetic boy of about sixteen.

This trip took us through some of the most beautiful waterways in the world but the highlight of this trip turned out to be one of the most hilariously funny things that I have ever seen. *It was at my grandson's expense of course.* It wouldn't have been nearly as funny if it had been mine.

It was about 4:00 AM when we pulled out of the driveway. All memorable outdoor trips start at 4:00 AM don't they? It would be about a five-hour trip, some of it spent on the British Columbia ferry system. It was shaping up to be a beautiful day. We were headed for what Canadians call their "*Sunshine Coast*" along the Straits of Georgia on the West mainland coast of British Columbia.

We were headed for a boat launch area on one of the inlets. It was a fjord not much unlike those in Norway. We had reserved two rental kayaks for our camping trip. These were salt-water kayaks, long skinny ones with a foot pedal rudder for steering. They were of very light fiberglass construction with a skirt that fit the paddler's waist to keep the water out. Each kayak had two small hatches to store gear.

"*Have you had any experience with kayaks?*" the lady asked. "*No,*" we answered. "*Well,*" she said, "*I'll give you some pointers eh,*" (In her Canadian accent). "First of all you have to learn how to get in one," she said. This was news to me. I thought all you had to do was jump in. Boy would I have been surprised. I was to soon find out that you could hardly reach up to scratch your ear without facing the perils of tipping the thing over. She then demonstrated how to get in. It was easy, at least for her. "Just put one end of the paddle on the bank," she said, "and the other end on the floating kayak and slide your butt along the paddle until you can drop in." Her demonstration made it look easy, but it was just sinking into my head how wobbly and unstable those kayaks really were. She then gave us the pointers on how to get out of the thing if it capsized. I didn't relish the thought at all. I'm not a good swimmer in the first place and second that water looked mighty cold to this old geezer. "Any questions?" she asked. "No," we answered pretending to be sure of ourselves.

We had a lot to learn, Dummy and I. The first thing we learned was that there was *no way* in hell we were going to get our camping gear in those two kayaks. The second thing we learned was that we were only going to get about *one-third* of our gear into those two kayaks.

It took awhile to sort through everything. We had to figure out how to stow just the bare essentials for a four-day kayak camping trip into the small compartments under each hatch. There would be no cooking on this trip. There certainly wasn't any room for our camp stove. We were able to take a little "*canned heat*" burner though so that we could have some hot coffee. In addition we stowed a six-by-eight foot tarp into each kayak along with food and water, sleeping bags, air mattresses and food. A change of clothes also for each of us. Now, finally, we were ready to go.

It was still fairly early in the morning when we pushed off. It was a wobbly start. Just getting into one of those things was an adventure. It took very little effort to make one of those things glide through the water but they sure are tippy. At first you're almost afraid to blink your eyes for fear of capsizing. These little boats are a nautical "wonder" though. At first I "*wondered*" if I was ever going to see my family again and I "*wondered*" why I had come up with such a crazy idea anyhow. I "*wondered*" what it would be like to thrash around under the thing in that cold, cold water if I capsized.

It only took three or four hours of paddling for us to gain confidence. We were old hands now as we put in on a small beach to eat our lunch. We had a new challenge. How do you get out of this thing without getting wet? "*I'll just let Dummy hit the beach first*", I thought. Maybe I can learn to get out of this thing by watching his mistakes.

It wasn't a graceful landing for sure. Not too bad though for our first try. It was a pleasant spot, peaceful and serene. It was a bright, sunny afternoon as we sat down to our gourmet lunch. Even soda crackers and cheese are gourmet foods when you're camping and we ate our fill.

Time to launch again. This time it was much easier. We had more confidence now and our push-off was a lot more graceful. By now, a strong wind had begun to blow out on the open water. We learned later that this was an everyday occurrence in the after-

Hey, these things glide along pretty good once you get the "hang of it"

noons. The wind was whipping up small swells with white caps. This made for some pretty scary paddling for us inexperienced kayakers. We soon learned that it was risky to get crosswise of the swells. The wind was a big help though for our progress. We could just coast along under wind power with very little energy expended on our part.

This inlet had several primitive campgrounds along the way. These were for boat access only. They were spread about every four or five miles. We had a little map with us showing all the campsites that the lady furnished with the kayaks. We had chosen a campsite and by the time we got there, it was already getting pretty well into the evening.

We paddled up to a little peninsula. It was just a little finger of land that jutted out into the water about three hundred feet and it was about a hundred feet wide. It had some clumps of brush on the slopes and at the water's edge, a few young trees were here and there but the top was open and grassy. Eventually we figured out that this little finger of land was man made, built most likely for the purpose of loading logs on barges or making up log rafts some fifteen or twenty years prior to our arrival. This was one of the designated campsites most likely chosen by the Canadian authorities because it was the only flat spot for miles around.

The Canadians are a hospitable people. We were *welcome* to camp at their site but apparently they just didn't want us to *sleep* there. Or maybe they just have a sense of humor because there for all to see on a big yellow sign were the words, "*Warning, Bear Area!*" That sign didn't need a whole lot of fine print. I could just use my imagination for the rest of it. This was our first night out. Who could sleep next to a sign like that?

It was a long night. The sign said nothing at all about more than one bear, but I could hear them everywhere. The people who put up that sign could have made an even bigger impact on my unrest had they added one word making it "*Warning, Hungry Bear Area*". They just don't know what an opportunity they had missed. If they had added the word "*hungry*" to that sign, I wouldn't have gotten any sleep at all. It's amazing how much a little raccoon or even a field mouse can sound like a great big black bear on a dark night in the wilderness.

We just had the bare essentials for camping with us, just a little food and a little "canned heat" burner for heating the coffee. For sleeping, we had our sleeping bags with air mattresses underneath on the ground to protect their undersides from the damp ground and as a cushion and we would pull the tarp over the top of us to keep out the dew.

It was a long night. It takes awhile to get used to the hard ground and the night noises. Morning welcomed us with a new chill in the air that always comes in late August. The sun was rising though. Its slowly increasing warmth and that first cup of hot coffee made us feel like we were living in the lap of luxury.

We had covered about twenty-five miles by the time we reached the end of the fjord. We had seen some beautiful scenery along the way. There were bright, colorful starfish clinging to the vertical rock walls at the water's edge. There were harbor seals, some with pups and all kinds of birds, mostly of the saltwater type. There were fish farms along the way too. These were underwater salmon pens where salmon are grown commercially. It appeared that workers would come out once each day in powerboats to feed them.

It was on our outbound trip that we learned another hard lesson about kayaking. We had already learned how easy it is to paddle along with the wind. Now we were to learn how doubly difficult it would be to face it. It was an easy trip inbound but we were going to have to fight for almost every inch of headway in the afternoons on the way out. The water was placid each day until about 10:00 AM. This made for easy paddling, but after ten o'clock, it was a different story. We would hug the shorelines and inlets as much as we could but it was still tough going.

The weather had changed. It looked like it was going to rain as we approached the last campsite for our last *"restful"* night. We didn't realize it yet, but this was going to be a night to remember.

There were a few drops of rain just beginning to fall by the time we finished our meal. We quickly laid out our air mattress and sleeping bags and covered them with the tarps. It was getting dusky by now under the trees. We could tell it was going to be a long, wet, hard night but we were counting on our tarps to keep us snug and dry. We had used a stick to scratch out little ditches around our sleeping bags to divert the surface water. At last, feeling secure, we crawled into our sleeping bags.

When the light rain fell at first, the forest canopy overhead was enough to protect us. As the night wore on, the rain increased. Soon the trees overhead reached their saturation point and started dripping water in huge drops. When these big drops splashed hard on these tarps in the quiet of the night they sounded like somebody was hitting them with a small stick, *splat, splash, splat.*

It was about 11:00 PM when I heard his first complaint. *"I'm cold,"* Josh said, *"and I'm getting wet."* "Just keep the tarp over you and you'll be OK, Shut up and go to sleep," I answered, unsympathetic to his plight. Only a few minutes went by and he was complaining again. *"I'm all wet Gramps,"* he complained, *"and I'm c-c-c-cold."* "Just keep the tarp over you and you'll be OK," I replied. "Go to sleep", I added. This went on and on until about 1:00 AM when he finally quieted down. I knew he was uncomfortable. I could hear him thrashing around under that tarp but even at home he slept like an old bear. His bed was almost always a scattered mess not very much unlike a rat's nest.

It was 2:00 AM now. Josh had been quiet for an hour and I began to worry about him. "I had better check on him, to see if he was OK", I thought. He could be in a state of hypothermia for all I knew. I was beginning to worry and thought I had better check to see if all was well. It had been raining hard all night. Maybe he'd drowned. I was going to catch hell from Grandma if she found out I wasn't taking good care of that boy.

It took awhile to fumble around in the dark to find my flashlight. I had to be careful to keep the tarp perfectly in place so that I wouldn't get wet from the rain. It was worth the trouble though because when I pointed that beam of light at Josh's bed, I was treated to one of the most hilarious scenes that I was ever to witness and one to long remember.

It was obvious even at first glance that he had worked his way down in his sleeping bag on the end of his air mattress. Even though he was under the tarp, I could tell that he was curled up in a heap. *What made the scene hilarious was that the air mattress was sticking out about two feet from under the tarp. It was slanting upward forming a perfect funnel.* It was really a sight to behold. I knew that Josh was probably miserable but I laughed anyway until my sides hurt and brought tears to my eyes. He had worked his way down in the sleeping bag to get away from the water and the deeper he got, all the more the funnel was catching the rain.

"*Wake up, Dummy*", I said, "*put that tarp back in place before you get wet.*" "*I'm already wet,*" came the reply, "*and I'm c-c-c-cold too.*" I could tell by his voice that he wasn't a happy camper.

It took him awhile to get his tarp all straightened out. I held the light on his space so he could see what he was doing. It was hard not to laugh at his plight. Every time I thought of that funnel shaped mattress I would burst out laughing but for some reason, he didn't think the whole thing was funny at all.

It was only about three more hours until daylight. I wasn't all that comfortable either but at least I was warm and dry and I thought I could get a little sleep.

Sleep was not to happen. Every time that I thought about that funnel it would make me laugh until my sides hurt. Josh would hear me laughing and would complain and grumble at me. The more he would grumble, the more I would laugh. Sleep was not to happen. The whole thing was just too funny. It makes me laugh now, nearly nine years later, just to think about it.

It was now about 4:00 AM. We had settled down a little bit. It was still raining though not quite as heavy. Suddenly, there was a big crash. We thought a bear was attacking us at first but soon realized it was a tree falling. We couldn't have been more than a hundred feet away from it and it really got our attention.

Josh was on his feet in a flash. By the time I got the flashlight trained on him he was already on his feet standing in the rain. *"That's it! I'm outta here!"* he said. I guess the sound of that tree crashing in the dark was the final straw for him. It was the final insult and he was headed out in no uncertain terms. *"But it's still dark!"* I said. I was still warm and dry. There was just no way that I wanted to get out of my sleeping bag. *"But it's still dark."* I tried again but he just wasn't in any mood to listen. *"I'm outta here, I'm heading home!"* he insisted. I knew that his mind was made up and I was just going to have to go along with it.

It only took a few minutes to pick up our gear and stow it in the kayaks and we were ready to launch. One last look around with the flashlight to make sure we hadn't missed anything and off we went into the dark waters of the fjord.

We had about a three-hour paddle before we would ever see the dock where our pickup truck was parked. I was still having laughing fits every time I thought about the night's events but we were going to make it somehow. It didn't really matter how much it rained now anyway because we were already wet and on the water. What difference could it possibly make? The considerable exertion it took to paddle the kayaks was enough to keep us quite warm even though we were quite wet from the rain.

It wasn't too bad at all once we were out on the water. I'm sure this was the first time that Josh had been warm since he had crawled into his sleeping bag the evening before. It's surprising how much light is reflected off the water even on the darkest night. We could actually see quite well. It was no trouble at all following the shoreline though we kept out in deeper water so that we wouldn't hit any hidden snags.

We met some powered fishing boats along the way, these were enclosed so rain was of no concern to their passengers. They had their navigation lights on making them very easy to see. It is very doubtful that the boatmen saw us at all in the dark. If they did, they most likely wondered what those two *lunatics in kayaks* were doing out there in the rain and in the dark. We didn't have any idea where those men in powerboats were going. Perhaps they were going up the fjord to feed the fish in those salmon pens we had passed a couple of days before.

It had become daylight at least an hour before we reached the dock. The rain had subsided quite a bit. Still the dock was a welcome sight as it slowly appeared directly ahead. The pickup truck was a welcome sight indeed because it held the dry clothes that we would soon climb into.

There were just a few more details before we could head home. There was a pay-phone nearby. First we had to call the lady to come for her kayaks and I called Joy to let her know that we were safely back in civilization. While waiting for the lady to come, we spent our time stowing our gear in the pickup and recounting the night's events. Eventually the lady came. We helped her load the kayaks on top of her pickup. That done, we headed for home.

Dummy and I had taken another trip at a lot earlier time, he was then about twelve years old. It was a camping trip too, *sort of.* I had been building a product for sometime that was called a S*eeboard.* These were used as a snorkeling alternative in the beach rental shops. As a result I had made contact with a business owner on Catalina Island just off the California coast near Los Angeles who needed some Seeboards delivered.

This too, was going to be a sort of camping trip, a very low budget trip, it was for sure. First thing to do was to build a plywood

A Seeboard on the beach in Hawaii

deck across the back of the pickup truck. This would be a platform on which to carry the Seeboards and of which I could sleep underneath at night. Josh, was going to sleep on the seat in the cab.

Off we went , on our little adventure, Dummy and I, it all worked out pretty good too, with just a few minor glitches otherwise. First of all, since we would be camping, we decided that we should take a scenic route, highway 395 was chosen as far as Reno, Nevada. Then across the Sierras to San Francisco and on south down the coast. It was the first night out when the first problem arose, at least for me anyway. We had picked a nice place along the highway for our camping spot under some pine trees and all was well. We had our snacks and now it was time to go to get some sleep. Josh crawled into his sleeping bag in the cab and got all snuggled in and I crawled in under the deck in the back. It was pretty close quarters under there, so it took quite a bit of squirming around to get settled in. First I had to reach back to pull the heavy tailgate up and slam it hard against the latch so that it would stay closed and then squirm around to get comfortably settled into my sleeping bag. It wasn't a bad arrangement really as camping goes and we settled in for a good night's sleep.

It wasn't until daybreak that a problem arose, it was time to get up and I couldn't get out from under the platform. I thought it was going to be easy but try as I might, I just couldn't get that tailgate unlatched. It was pretty claustrophobic under that deck to start with and finding myself trapped under there didn't make it any easier at all. The small space that I had to put my arm through under the deck just didn't allow for me to get enough leverage to unlock that stubborn latch. I was trapped like a raccoon in a box trap while raiding the hen-house.

I was beginning to get desperate now, for one thing nature was calling severely and panic was starting to set in. I'm just going to have to wake *Dummy* to unlatch the tailgate from the outside, I decided as I crawled forward under the deck. Well I soon found that wasn't going to be easy. *Even at home Dummy slept like Rip Van Winkle* and on this particular morning he was really sawing the old logs. "*Dummy*", I yelled, "*wake up*", no reply, "*wake up*", I might as well have tried to wake the dead for all the good my efforts were doing! No matter how hard I tried, I couldn't get even the slightest response from him. My bladder was starting to scream at my kidneys now, I was really getting desperate. "*Dummy, wake up*", I yelled some more, still no response, kicking and thumping the front of the pickup box didn't seem to be doing a whole lot of good either.

The predicament I was in now was getting more desperate by the moment, *my bladder* was saying to my kidneys, "*I want a divorce, I just can't take it any more*", it screamed, "*I just cant take it any more*"! They were ready to "duke it out" and their battle was getting worse by the moment.

Well finally, after much ranting and raving, Josh roused from his sleep, it took a little while for him to figure out what I needed. Even then he didn't seem to be in much of a hurry and even seemed to find the whole thing kind of amusing. Perhaps he may have been trying to "*get even*" for some of the *tricks* that I had pulled on him in the past.

It was quite easy for him to open the tailgate from the outside and once freed from my trap I headed for the bushes in a hurry just as the raccoon would do back at the "hen-house".

It was in a Reno grocery store that I saw a chance to teach Josh a lesson about economics, I wanted to show him the foolishness of gambling. There was a row of slot machines near the bagging area and in my "*great wisdom*" I knew that if I gave him a couple of dollars for the slots, he would lose it all in just a few seconds. It would be a good lesson, I thought, about the folly of gambling. Well it took only a few seconds to pop the money in those slots and much to my dismay he about doubled his money on the first try. Normally this wouldn't be a problem because with continued play the money would be gone and a lesson learned. Well it was not to be, immediately I was cornered by the store manager and chewed out for abetting a minor in gambling. *I lost out all around, I lost the money I had invested for the object lesson, had gotten chewed out real good and the lesson had gone awry.*

We were having a great adventure, Dummy and I, the weather was perfect, it was a beautiful day. We had just crossed over the Sierra Nevada mountains and Lake Tahoe was coming into view. "Can we go swimming Grandpa" Dummy asked, "sure I think it would be fun", I replied.

Lake Tahoe is a huge lake with a lake shore of many miles, even so after passing many coves, my twelve year old passenger was getting impatient. He wanted to go swimming and in his eyes "*old Gramps*" wasn't cooperating very well at all. After passing many coves Josh started to pout, "we're going to be all the way past the lake pretty soon", *he pouted,* sticking his lower lip out so far it began to look like a "*bird feeder*"."Oh don't worry, we'll stop pretty soon", I told him, "just as soon as we find a good place".

We finally came to a good looking spot to turn off down to the lake shore. We followed the gravel road in towards the lake about two hundred yards and "sure enough", there, right in front of us was a very nice beach. There were a lot of people wandering around on the beach and we soon found out why there weren't many in the water. The water was as cold as a "*well digger's butt*", it was cold "*brrr*", those mountain lakes are really cold.

We didn't stay in the water very long, it was just too cold. Josh lasted longer than I did but not very long, he soon began to feel the cold. If one was to stay in that water very long, one would look like one of those little blue "*smurf*" toys that the kids play with. "*The water's c-c-c-cold Gramps*", he said, "*it's too c-c-c-c-cold*", he complained.

The rest of our trip was pretty ordinary, though the camping options became very limited. There are just too many people down there in Southern California for good camping. Their idea of a good camp site is a forty acre paved parking lot with rest rooms and hose bibs scattered throughout. You can hardly find a tree any place to park in the shade, as a result we spent many nights parked under bridges etc..

A boat ride across the water to Catalina Island was memorable and the Island visit was a pleasant experience. We were able to swim among the kelp and the bright red Gerabaldi fish that abound there.

We were only gone from home about ten days in all but returned very satisfied with our little camping adventure.

Chapter 25

Winding Down

It seemed like hardly any time at all until those two little girls went off to college. Soon, they were followed by Dummy as well. I was finding the work more difficult year by year. *I was getting to be an old dog now.* I was fast losing the bounce in my *"leaper spring"*. I was getting gray around the muzzle too. I began to consider that if the younger dogs wanted the bone, they could just have it. *It was time for me to just sit on the porch and dream about my puppy years.*

About the same time that Dummy left for college, a friend of mine retired from a job in one of the local school districts. He loved outdoor work, landscaping in particular so we teamed up. He loved the hard work of landscaping and still does. He was one of the best men I ever worked with. His work ethic and everything else he did was above reproach and with a lot of class. As time wore on, he did more and more of the hardest work and I did less and less. I hung in there for a good while but finally it was apparent to me that it was time for me to retire. It was time for me to quit leaning on the shovel and just put it away along with all the other landscaping tools. *It was time to give up the bone to the younger dogs.* It was time to face the reality that my working years were all behind me. It was time to rest.

Chapter 26

How I Wondered
Where I Wandered

Now that I am an "*old geezer*", I have plenty of time to look back. Would I change anything if I had a second chance? Perhaps some, but not most things. What would I have to write about today if my life had always been safe and secure? What of the interesting people I have met? What experiences would I be really willing to do without?

I was short on formal education, but still I'm just like most everyone else, well schooled by experience, hard knocks and the vicissitudes of life. It's true that my spelling and grammar are not great but why should it be when you consider that those from higher learning have the language all screwed up in the first place? How many centuries will it take for all the professors to unscrew it, lest they should brag? Give me a really good reason why the word "*phone*" is spelled the way it is, or "*pneumonia*" or "*pneumatic*" or "*pneumoperitoneum*". If this makes any sense at all, then why not call a stone a "*wrock*" or my car a "*whreak*" or I'm moving into a "*pnew*" house, or that monster was a real *"phreak"*.

Even the simplest of numbers are screwed up. I've wondered about that too. Makes pretty good sense up to ten but it gets all messed up after that. Let's start with eleven. Seems to me that it should have been called *"onedy-onedy"*. The rest aren't too bad up to twenty but how about first, second and third. Seems to me that *"oneth"; "twonth "threeth"* would make more sense. How about changing *"twenty"* to *"twooty"* or thirty to *"threety"*.

For us, I guess it would sound strange to hear the teacher say to her *"twonth"* class for the day. "Class, if you add *twooty* and *threety* and subtract *onedy-onedy*, the sum will be *threety* nine."

Have you ever noticed that city people who live in a concrete jungle and have rarely seen a small running stream , call it a *creek*. Correctly so, I guess but why do country people who live right beside the running water call it a *crick*. Seems to me that the country people should be more knowledgeable about what it should be called, don't you agree?

Yes, it does seem that the masters of higher learning have everything all screwed up but I guess I'll just have to learn to live with it. I can't imagine anyone would want me to make the changes.

Chapter 27

The Last Chapter

In my lifetime I have "rubbed shoulders" with all kinds of characters, people from a lot of different cultures, from poor to rich, from smart to dull. I know that at least some of my personality must have "rubbed" off on them. It is my hope that only my better qualities made much of an impact.

I know that I made an impact on the character of at least one young man. It all happened on a dark night near our rural mail box. It was common in this area at the time for juveniles to smash mailboxes as a prank. Not too different really from the youths of my generation tipping the *"out houses"* over as a prank on Halloween, I guess. I had heard some rather loud voices out on the highway and thought I should investigate. As I went out the back door and walked around the side of the house, I could hear the mailboxes being attacked. It was dark, very dark but as I approached the road an image of two people could be seen against the glow in the sky from the city lights of the town nearby. Normally I am not a man who looks for a fight and I hate violence but these guys really made me mad. It only took about ten quick steps to close the gap. One of the guys saw me at the last instant and ran but the other one was too occupied mutilating the mailbox to notice. In just seconds I had him by the throat from behind, I'm sure that he thought that he was being attacked by an angry bear. "*What the hell do you think you're doing*"? I asked, "*urghk*", he replied as I tightened my grip on his throat. I questioned him some more about his *ancestry* while tightening my grip a little harder and lifting him up on his "tiptoes" but he only acknowledged the conversation with a couple more "*urghks*". "You had better get the hell out of here in a hurry when I turn you loose", I added, "*urghk, urghk*", he replied.

His feet were already moving as I let him down and turned him loose, it sure didn't take him very long to disappear into the darkness. I can imagine that his buddy was waiting for him out there somewhere and they had a lot to talk over when they got back together.

I don't know how old he was but I'm guessing that he may have been about sixteen. I know it wasn't a girl because *I had felt his adam's apple pinching my fingers*. I would guess that he may have weighed about one-hundred-fifty pounds or so.

If you chance on to a man some day and try to make some light conversation with him and all he has to say is "*urghk*" and "*urghk, urghk*", you'll know he was the guy tearing up the mailbox. We only *danced together* for a few moments but I'm sure I must have made a *lasting impression* on his character and personality.

How we are affected by the places we've been and the characters we have met is the premise of this book. I believe that we are part and parcel of everyone we've ever met and the places that we've ever been.

My character, I believe, started with the seeds of genetics but a much larger impact was made by the characters that I have rubbed shoulders with. *Most times, I was enriched tremendously* by those characters and sometimes, *I was just contaminated.* Still, I know of no other forces that effected me more.——————— *May it ever be so!*

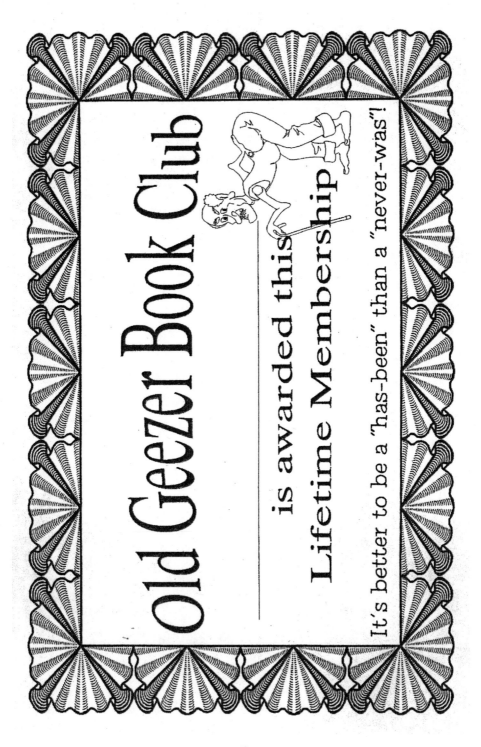

Old Geezer Book Club

is awarded this

_____

Lifetime Membership

It's better to be a "has-been" than a "never-was"!

Other books by Raymond C. Evans
"The Old Geezer"

Guts, Oats, Steam, Gasoline, Diesel & Spit

When Fast Food was a Rabbit

———

CONTACT:
Old Geezer Books
8813 Old Hwy 99 SE
Olympia, WA 98501
(360) 943-2188

WEB: http://www.oldgeezerbooks.com